Sophocles' *Antigone*.

A Study Guide

Table of contents

Sophocles' *Antigone*:

A Study Guide

Introductory Notes: Sophocles' *Antigone*: A Study Guide

Sophocles' *Antigone*

Antigone is a play that primarily concerns itself with the *polis*; the city. How should those in power act? Is it right to question their authority? What steps should be taken against those that challenge the established authority of the city?

Sophocles produced the Antigone around the year 443/2BC. The years immediately before and after were a period of tremendous activity and importance for the development of Athens and her empire and also significant for the author of the play himself, as he was closely involved with several of these events.

Studying GCE Classics

This critical study guide has been written to provide a rewarding experience for those who are studying Ancient Greek Civilization. In particular, this study guide will assist in understanding and examining Sophocles' *Antigone* in the wider context of Greek tragedy and the Athenian society in which it was produced and first performed.

This study guide is also suitable for those interested in Greek Tragedy for the enjoyment of the plays themselves. After all, Greek Tragedy is one of the world's great achievements and within Greek Tragedy are the origins of many of the great literary works which were produced and are still being written today.

Who is this study guide for?

This study guide is intended to offer a satisfying experience for those learners who undertake an AS or A level qualification in Classical Civilization. This qualification is currently offered by both AQA and OCR examination boards and this resource is primarily designed to assist those who are studying for this qualification. This study guide will also help to laying a sound foundation for those who go on to study the Ancient World at a higher (degree) level as well as appeal to those who are interested in learning more about the ancient world.

Please note however that these specifications are currently outgoing and new specifications are set to launch for first teaching in September 2017.

Sophocles' Antigone is also a play on the AQA A Level in Drama and Theatre as such this study guide will be of some assistance to learners of this A level course.

Please note that this study guide is not endorsed either by AQA or OCR and as such is not an officially recognised product by Edexcel, AQA, OCR or CIE examination boards.

It is however designed to be used as a study aide in order for learners to attain a qualification in the following A Level examination units;

- **OCR Classical Civilisation (2008 Specification)**

  F384 – Greek Tragedy in its context

- **AQA Classical Civilisation (2008 Specification)**

  CIV3C – Greek Tragedy

- **AQA – Drama and Theatre**

Translations of Sophocles' *Antigone*

The 'set text' recommended by the AQA and OCR examination boards is the following;

Sophocles' *Antigone* translated by R Fagles (Penguin)

However, OCR state that ANY complete translation of Sophocles' *Antigone* may be used to study for this unit.

Free versions of the play can be obtained from;

The Internet Classics Archive

www.classics.mit.edu/Sophocles/antigone.html

The Perseus digital Library

www.perseus.tufts.net

The Internet Classics Archive

http://classics.mit.edu/Browse/index.html

PiT – Poetry in Translation website

www.poetryintranslation.com

Both Kindle and iBooks also may offer free or purchasable versions of Sophocles' *Antigone* which may be used to accompany this study guide.

How to use this guide

This A Level study guide has been organised in such a way so as to help an A Level student of Ancient Greek Theatre more easily understand the life and career of Sophocles and his play *Antigone*. It has also been designed to correspond to the major topic areas identified by the major examination boards.

To this end this Athena Critical Guide is divided into *sections* that relate to a particular aspect or theme relating to the *Antigone*.

Each section is introduced with a number of bullet points that will help the reader to identify the focus of the section and also to help correlate the section to their relevant examination specification.

Within sections are a number of tasks and activities as well as glossary terms and additional points of information that are considered useful to an A Level student.

The tasks and activities are based on the structure and duration of questions posed by the examination boards therefore it is envisaged that they will be especially valuable in aiding the reader to prepare for their respective examinations.

Part One:

A Brief introduction to Greek Tragedy

1.1 Sophocles

This section consists of a brief introduction to Sophocles, the 5th century Athenian, Playwright and sometime General.

This section will help you to;

- *Understand briefly the three Greek Tragedians of 5th century Athens*

- *Explore the life and career of Sophocles*

- *Consider some of the styles and innovations introduced by Sophocles*

Aeschylus, Sophocles and Euripides: The Greek Tragedians.

Throughout the 5th century BC hundreds of tragedies were written in Greece by many different playwrights. However, the only complete plays that survive were written by three tragedians: Aeschylus, Sophocles and Euripides. All of these authors were Athenian and although their plays were later reproduced in many theatres across the Greek world, they were all produced initially for an Athenian audience in the city of Athens.

Aeschylus as the earliest surviving playwright wrote over seventy plays, of which only seven survive. Sophocles wrote one hundred and twenty three plays, of which seven also survive, and Euripides wrote ninety two plays, and of these nineteen survive. It is apparent then that the majority of plays have been lost entirely, or is available only in fragmentary form, preserved by other writers from the Greek and Roman period as quotations.

The lives of these three tragedians covered just over a hundred years, though their careers overlapped each other. Aeschylus was born in the 520s BC and died in 456 BC. Sophocles was born in the 490s BC and died in 406 BC. Euripides was born in the 480s BC and died just shortly before Sophocles. The careers of these three great writers cover the fifth century BC, a period which saw the flourishing of tragedy as an art form as well as the rise and fall of the Athenian Empire.

Sophocles

Sophocles was born at some time in the 490s BC, possibly in 496BC at the Attic town of Colonus and died in 406BC.

He competed for over sixty years in the *City Dionysia* (from 468-406 BC), with his first prize coming on his first attempt in 468BC. For such a long career it is no surprise that Sophocles wrote over one hundred and twenty three plays however only seven have survived. Of Aeschylus, Sophocles and Euripides, Sophocles was by far the most successful of the three. In the course of his career Sophocles achieved victory over twenty times with eighteen of these at the *City Dionysia*. According to ancient commentators Sophocles never came last at the *City Dionysia*.

Sophocles was also a prominent politician and at least occasionally active participant in the Athenian Democracy. He served as a *Hellenotamiae* (A Greek treasurer responsible for the funds of the Athenian Empire) in 443/2BC. This also provides a clue as to the nature of Sophocles' background as only the wealthiest Athenian citizens could serve as a *Hellenotamiae*.

Sophocles was also elected as a *Strategos*, a General in 441BC and commanded soldiers at the siege of the island of Samos in that year alongside the premier Athenian statesman of the day, Pericles. According to ancient commentators, Sophocles was appointed General in part due to his victory at the *City Dionysia* with the play *Antigone*. He may have also been a specialist advisor appointed by the state during the Peloponnesian War, when Athens suffered a great military disaster in Sicily in 413BC.

Of Sophocles' seven surviving plays only two can be dated with certainty;

- *Philoctetes* (409BC)

- *Oedipus at Colonus* (407/6BC - achieving a posthumous victory in 401 BC)

- *Ajax*

- *Antigone*

- *Oedipus King*

- *Women of Trachis*

Antigone is thought to have been written towards the end of the 440s, whilst Oedipus the King has been attributed to coincide with the plague that affected Athens in 430/429BC. These are sensible guesses, but they are not for certain.

Sophocles the innovator

Sophocles is credited with introducing the 3rd Actor into Greek tragedy. By adding a 3rd actor Sophocles helped to contribute to character interaction and development in the complexity of the drama. Two actors could discourse but by adding a third the complexity of the plot of the play could be become much more developed. Imagine the *Antigone* without Ismene when Creon interrogates Antigone, or the Messengers at the end of the play. The play would lose a great detail of its depth and intensity.

1.2 An introduction to Greek Tragedy

This section will help you to;

- *Explore the difference between the ancient Greek and modern theatre.*

- *Identify what a Greek Theatre looked like and consider some of its components*

- *Consider the nature of dramatic festivals and competitions in 5th century Athens.*

- *Explain the deployment and use of some of the stage machinery and theatre buildings.*

Comparing the ancient and modern theatre

Despite having its roots in Ancient Greek theatre, modern theatre is very different. First of all modern theatre is primarily for entertainment. In contrast Athenian theatre productions, although they were entertaining and engaging for the audience, were an integral part of Athenian religious festivals that were designed to unite the Athenian citizen body as well as honouring the gods.

Modern-day theatre audiences of theatre tend to be largely directed towards the middle classes of society with the majority of audiences being comprised of adults. However the range of theatre on offer can and does have the capability of attracting a broad spectrum of people of all ages and from all sections of society. In 5th century Athens the audience was primarily if not entirely male. Whether women did or did not attend is still debated.

Another difference between the ancient and modern is that the modern audience would only expect to see one play at a time. In Athens at the festivals were they were performed the audience would watch several plays in a row; all by the same author and often interconnected. Perhaps the closest modern comparison would be to view a trilogy of films in succession such as the Star Wars trilogy.

A modern audience also expect and choose to go to the theatre at any time during the year. In London's West End for example are a wide range of plays, some of which have been performed day on day for years. A typical ancient Athenian citizen would only see a play in relation to a religious festival on a limited number of days each year. As can be seen then, the ancient and modern experience of theatre varied enormously. Some plays were written to reflect upon current events and when read as literary works it is important to always bear in mind how they were intended to be received by their original audiences, and in what context they were performed.

Characteristics of the Greek theatre

The design of ancient Greek Theatres is iconic and today modern cinemas and theatre halls still greatly resemble those initial theatres designed and built by the Ancient Greeks.

Theatres were constructed outdoors and to a similar design, several of these theatres still survive today with the most famous being the theatres at Athens and Epidavros, which attract thousands of tourists each year. These theatres are still in use and it is possible to see plays performed in them through the summer in Greece.

Theatre performances were probably constricted to a few special occasions a year. However smaller theatres at small towns such as Brauron in Attica were probably used by the local town councils for meetings also. Some theatres could accommodate a large number of people; the theatre of Dionysus in Athens for example can hold up to 14,000 people, as could the theatre at Epidavros.

Theatre going was not an activity limited to a particular social class. All ancient Greeks viewed theatre going as an activity open to them. However it is probable that women were excluded from some performances or the seating and had to content themselves with viewing the performances from a distance.

Greek tragedy conformed to certain genre expectations: it was staged on a vast scale, and took as its subject matter the ancient Greek myths as a starting point. The audience watching a tragedy were taking part in a communal experience since the subject on stage was based on their shared cultural heritage.

The Theatre

The Greek theatre is easily identifiable as an outdoor structure of semi-circle design. The audience sat on tiers in a semi-circle around a circular performance area, called an *orchestra*. There were two exits or entrances opposite the audience, leading to a building (*skené*) which incorporated a stage platform and a roofed structure. This was the only roofed construction in the entire theatre: it served as a changing space for the cast of the play, but also where necessary could stand for a palace, house (as in the case of *Electra*) or even a forest. Each play would also utilise props and scenic furniture as appropriate.

The design of a Greek theatre of an angled semi-circle was intentional. The acoustics of the design were so good, that if you dropped a coin in the orchestra, then the highest audience member sitting on the top tier might be able to hear it. Today, many tourists create impromptu speeches at the theatre of Epidavros which can be clearly heard by all present within the theatre. In modern film the emphasis is often on the visual impact of the film. In Ancient Greece it was most important that everybody could *hear* the play.

A vase painting depicting a *skené*

Stage Machinery

The stage machinery used in the Ancient Greek theatre was fairly simplistic. Trapdoors were used for actors to access the stage from below. One of the main pieces of machinery was a large crane, called a *mechané*. The *mechané* was used to 'swing' actors and thus give the impression that they were flying. This was used especially when the play incorporated a god. If the god did not stand atop the *skéné* (stage building) or in the orchestra, then they could be moved around by the *mechané* to give the impression of flight.

Another important piece of equipment was the *ekkyklema*, a kind of wheeled, moveable platform that could be rolled on stage to display something; typically a 'dead' body.

Athenian Dramatic Festivals

In common with the other kinds of theatrical genres of ancient Greece; tragedy was performed as part of a religious festival or ceremony in honour of the god, Dionysus. In this ancient and modern theatre are greatly at odds, the ancient theatre and religion were inexorably intertwined.

Tragedy, alongside the other genres, was performed only at two major festivals every year.

The first, in Athens, was the **City Dionysia,** which took place over a few days in spring. The tragedies and the other types of theatre were performed as part of a mass competition in honour of the God Dionysus. This was a grand occasion; normal business was suspended and all citizens attended the festival for the purpose of watching the theatre on offer. Visitors from across the Greek world would also attend.

The second, the **Lenaia**, taking place probably earlier in the year, in January, was a less important festival. Although the festival was still to honour the god Dionysus, the plays performed tended towards comedy, rather than tragedy.

Both festivals were important religious events and the Athenian state took a great role and pride in preparing these enterprises. A senior official, called an *archon*, was put in charge of the *City*

Dionysia and chose the three separate poets whose works would be entered for performance. He was also in charge of finding and allocating the actors.

The Nature of competition at the *City Dionysia*

The three successful playwrights chosen by the *archon* in advance of the Great Dionysia were each allotted a *choregos*, or a rich citizen, whose role was to finance the production personally. The role of *choregos* was a voluntary form of civic duty undertaken by rich citizens as an alternative form of taxation; they could chose this role or that of equipping the Athenian navy as another way of performing the functions required of the city-state of Athens.

However, there were benefits for a *choregos* besides paying his taxes: spending money on a lavish and exciting new production would confer fame on him and hopefully would garner him popularity as well. For rich citizens with an eye on their political status on a public stage, this could be extremely useful. In other cities that did not have the resources of festivals of Athens, the rich would compete and demonstrate their wealth through the ownership of horses and chariot racing teams as well as other spectacles, including provision of public buildings or dedications to the gods.

The Great Dionysia took place over five days. On three days of the festival, one playwright would present a trilogy of tragedies followed by a 'satyr' play, which was a kind of light-hearted farce, named after the mythological creature of the satyr. The three plays in the tragedy may have been linked by theme or not, but the only surviving complete trilogy we have is that of Aeschylus' *Oresteia*. This is composed of the plays *Agamemnon*, *Choephori* and *Eumenides*. A comedy would also be performed the same day.

The theatre of Dionysius at Athens

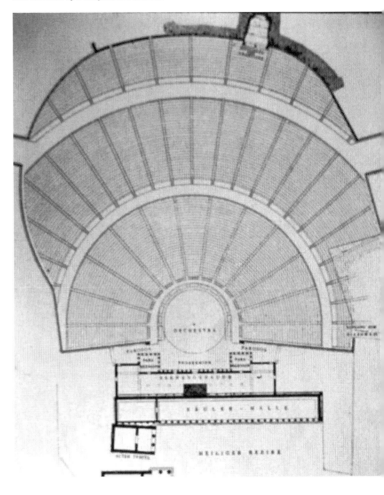

The Structure of Greek Tragedy

Most dramas open with a *Prologue* as monologue. In the case of *Women of Troy* it is the speech of Poseidon that begins the play. After the *Prologue*, usually the chorus enters and offers the *first* of the choral songs called the *Parados*. In the case of *Women of Troy* for example, Euripides inserts the first episode, consisting of the dialogue between Poseidon and Athena, between the *Prologue* and the *Parados*. The final scene is called the *Exodos*.

The structure of Greek Tragedies often resembles the following;

Prologue

Parados (Strophé / Antistrophé/ Epodé)

First Episode

First Stasimon (Strophé / Antistrophé/ Epodé)

Second Episode

Second Stasimon (Strophé / Antistrophé/ Epodé)

Third Episode

Third Stasimon (Strophé / Antistrophé/ Epodé)

Fourth Episode

Fourth Stasimon (Strophé / Antistrophé/ Epodé)

Exodus

1.3: The role and function of the Chorus and Actors

This section will help you to;

- *Explain the use of the Chorus and actors in Greek tragedy.*

- *Explain ancient Greek dramatic terminology and conventions for both Chorus and actors.*

- *Understand three key concepts of Greek Tragedy as defined by Aristotle.*

The Use of the Chorus

The Chorus is a distinctive and perhaps the most important feature of the Greek Tragedy. The Chorus formed a centerpiece of the spectacle at the festival of Dionysius at Athens. Many plays, both comic and tragic, take their name from the chorus; For example plays with the titles of *Women of Troy, Knights, Birds* and *Bacchae*.

To raise and train a Chorus was considered to be a great public duty and honour. As a result of the expense involved it was the wealthiest citizens who could afford to do this. The *chorégos* (Chorus leader) recruited, trained and costumed the chorus.

Despite the shift to an increased number of actors with speaking parts, the Chorus was an integral part of the drama and spectacle of a tragedy. The Chorus was made up of fifteen members, including a Chorus leader. Originally there were twelve members of a tragic chorus, later in the 5th century this was increased to fifteen. In contrast, comedies had a twenty four strong chorus and fifty in the chorus for a dithyramb.

The Chorus performed by dancing, singing and speaking either in unison, in groups or individually through the Chorus leader, who might speak directly to the actors on stage. Besides these functions the Chorus served other important roles in the play. The dialogue or monologue spoken by the main actors, usually called 'episodes', was often punctuated by the choral songs or dances. This allowed the action to be slowed and indicate the passing of time, to act as 'scene changes' or to allow for a change of mood. They would also interject with lines in the dialogue of the main actors.

Furthermore, the choral songs allowed for some added variety to the format of the tragedy; the Chorus sang in a different type of verse to the spoken parts and so allowed the tragedian to demonstrate his skills of versification. These songs were often timed to the movement of the chorus about the performance area.

These lines, known as *strophé* and *antistrophé* ended with turns in direction made by the chorus as they sang and danced. These 'turns' and 'counterturns', combined with song were an important in the context of performance; the tragedies were performed as part of a competition sacred to Dionysus and impressing the judges and audience was therefore paramount.

The Use of Actors in Greek Tragedy

The total number of actors with speaking parts started at one, and grew to two, finally stopping at three. A reason for limiting the number to three was probably practical. The audience may have been too distracted by too much occurring on stage at once and by several parts being played by the same actor who wore masks to identify these characters probably made additional speaking actors unnecessary.

Aristotle credited Aeschylus with adding the second actor and Sophocles with the third actor. This did not mean that tragedies had to be written with only three speaking parts; actors took more than one part. Besides the speaking parts, Greek tragedy also made use of walk-on, non-speaking parts, such as guards and slaves. In the *Antigone* for example a boy accompanies Tiresias on stage and is commented upon; yet has no lines.

The role of the speaking or non-speaking parts, played by single actors grew in importance as the number of speaking-part actors was increased to three. This leads us to consider the other stage presence in Greek tragedy; the Chorus.

Features of Greek Tragedy

Below are a number of key terms that all learners of Greek Theatre should be familiar with.

Rhesis

This is the name given to a set speech by an actor which is characterised by logical argument or ordered reasoning, yet may also include emotional appeal. It could be a monologue, where a character reflects on his opinions, feelings and motivations, or it could be part of a dialogue or argument. It is a common feature of Greek Tragedy.

Stichomythia

This is a particular kind of argument or dialogue, consisting of a rapid, single-line exchange. It is not the only kind of dialogue in tragedy, but is of a highly distinctive kind. It serves to concentrate and heighten the emotion or argument, since the exchange frequently takes place between two characters of opposing view-points or of wildly different intentions.

Agon

A debate. One character presents his or her case, in a formal manner, and another character refutes the points made. It has the feel of the 'law-court' about them. The aim is to capture the audience through reasoned argument, and since tragedies often represent the clash of two opposing ideologies, there is much food for thought to be found in the *agon*.

Kommos

It is a lament. Often a *kommos* is a lyrical exchange between the Chorus and a character.

The Messenger speech

In contrast to the reasoned argument characteristic of the *rhesis* or the *agon*, the messenger speech makes full use of appeal to the audience's emotions. These speeches are used as a reporting device of the tragedians, and allowed them to describe the violence vividly, a consequence of their characters' actions, without breaking the taboo of representing violence on-stage. The messenger speeches take the form of narrative; a messenger arrives to report on what he has seen take place out of sight of the audience.

Dramatic Conventions used in Greek Tragedy

Below are a number of conventions that all learners of Greek Theatre should be familiar with.

Offstage action

Greek tragedy also involved elements that were absent from the stage and performance area and yet were integral parts of the plot. In the *Antigone,* for example, the suicides of Antigone, Haemon and Eurydice do not occur in view of the audience. Graphic killings on stage were considered taboo at a religious festival. Nonetheless they need to happen and so Antigone uses other methods and techniques in order to inform the audience of these events.

Examples of Tragic episodes and the demonstration of these events that occur 'off-stage';

- **Cries**

    In several plays including *Ajax, Medea* and *Electra* a character may be heard crying or screaming off stage. This is used to increase tension.

- **Violence**

    The portrayal of violence was taboo at a religious festival. Several Greek tragedies have violent episodes, including this one – but they are not portrayed onstage. When Clytemnestra and Aegisthus are murdered in *Electra*; it is done off stage and reported to the actors, chorus and audience by use of a Messenger.

- **Description of events that occur elsewhere**

    Sometime news is delivered of important events; such as the mysterious burial of the dead in *Antigone*. In this case the event is usually described by a Messenger, guard or other witness who comes on stage briefly to inform the actors and chorus of these distant events.

Iambic pentameter

The verse form of Greek Tragedy was a fundamental feature of the genre. The actors spoke in a type of verse called iambic pentameter, since this was considered to be the closest to normal speech. It has a rhythm of uniform metre that resembled *'te-tum, te-tum, te-tum'* in sound.

Lyric poetry; *strophe, antistrophe* and *epode*

In origin lyric poetry and dance were an integral part of religious ceremony.

However, the choral songs were quite different, which marked again marked them off from the main spoken action. The type of poetry they sang in was called lyric poetry, and was of a far more complex kind than the verse of the actors with speaking parts.

Choral songs were composed of three elements or *'stanzas'*. These stanzas consisted of a number of turns and counterturns (*strophé* and *antistrophé*) as well as a different paced final *stanza* called the *'epode'*, which was of a different metrical pattern to the other two stanzas.

Costume and Masks

Besides the theatre building, scene machinery and Chorus there were many other distinct features of Greek tragedy. All actors wore costumes and masks, although it is difficult to know exactly what design or type these took.

The masks were of rigid construction, with an aperture (opening) for the mouth. These masks were worn for a variety of reasons; firstly, the design of the theatre itself necessitated them. The aperture may have acted as a sound amplifier, helping the audience to hear the words he spoke or sang. The mask was also an exaggerated face and so would help the audience in the highest seats distinguish one part from another. The masks would also be in the form of stereotypes of stock characters, such as a King, an old man or a noble woman. This had the effect of clarifying from a distance which character was which.

Key concepts of Greek tragedy as defined by Aristotle;

These three terms, used by Aristotle in his work on the nature of Greek tragedy, called the *Poetics,* are very useful to our understanding of tragedy. These are;

- *Hamartia*

- *Catharsis*

- *Peripeteia*

- *Anagnorisis*

Hamartia

Hamartia derives from a Greek root word meaning 'to miss the mark' or 'to fall short'. In the context of Greek tragedy, *hamartia* refers to a failing of the central character which brings out the catastrophe. It has sometimes been translated as a 'character flaw'; but this is to fall short of the true meaning of the word.

In fact, it is not so much an in-grained character fault as more an opportunity missed, or bad decision made which sets up the inescapability and inevitability of the tragic events which follow. Each of the tragedies we study will contain this 'falling short' or *hamartia* of the central character, and will be considered in our close reading of the text.

An example of *harmatia* in *Antigone* is the short comings of Creon. He comes across as arrogant and bullying and yet finally indecisive. It is down the urgings of the Chorus that he is finally resolved to take pity on Antigone.

Katharsis

Katharsis gives us our word 'cathartic' which we use to refer to something with a great cleansing or purging power. The word in the context of Greek tragedy refers to the effect a 'good' tragedy should have on the audience. It should purge the audience of its emotions, by inducing feelings such as pity, anger or fear and allowing the audience a safe place for the expression of them.

A cathartic event in the Euripides' *Electra* is the appearance of the Dioscoûri at the end of the play. Both Orestes and Electra are contaminated by their actions. They need to be cleansed and the gods explain how this can be achieved. As we will investigate in this study guide of *Antigone*, the play may or may not have *Katharsis*.

Peripeteia

Peripeteia refers to a (usually sudden) reversal or change of fortune of the central character. Again, like *hamartia* this is a typical feature of a Greek tragedy. The reversal can be from good to bad or vice versa. Aristotle considered the first, the change from happiness to misery, the more significant for tragedy.

Creon rapidly undertakes a reversal of fortunes in *Antigone*. He arrives on stage a King making laws and demands; he exits the play a broken man with no family.

Anagnorisis

Anagnorisis effectively means recognition. It is the point in a tragedy when a character recognises or discovers the true nature of the situation or true identity of another character. According to Aristotle all good tragedies should have a moment of Anagnorisis

Part Two:

Sophocles' *Antigone*

2.1: Sophocles' *Antigone:* Background and Context

Introduction

This topic focuses on introducing one of the most dynamic and 'modern' of all Greek tragedies for modern audiences, Sophocles' *Antigone*.

In this section we will;

- *Explore the mythological background to the Antigone*

- *Investigate the historical and political context of the play*

- *Understand the characters of the play*

- *Consider the structure of the play*

The Mythological background to the *Antigone*

Set in Thebes, *Antigone* shares a common scene for Tragic Plays. Thebes featured in Sophocles' *Oedipus the King*, *Oedipus at Colonus* as well as Aeschylus' *Seven against Thebes* as well as Euripides' *Phoenissae*. Thebes was in 5th century BC Greece, the largest city of Boeotia, a region in central mainland Greece that neighboured Attica, which was in turn the home of Athens.

According to the Mythic tradition, the city of Thebes was founded by Cadmus, a man born in Phoenicia, a region placed in modern day Lebanon/Israel. Once in Boeotia, Cadmus confronted and killed a Dragon at the site of what would become Thebes. Cadmus then ploughed the ground and sowed the ground with the teeth of the dragon, these teeth grew into fully armed warriors and it was these 'Dragon Men' that became the noble families of Thebes.

Laius

Time passed and Laius became king of Thebes, but unfortunately Laius had been cursed as a child. This curse would tragically work its' magic on Laius and his descendants for the next two generations, and in doing so, would provide the Ancient Greeks with some of their most evocative myths.

Laius and his wife Jocasta were told that their new-born son would kill Laius. In order to prevent this fate, Laius and Jocasta decided to abandon the baby on the slopes of Mount Cithaeron to die. This baby did not die however; he was rescued by a shepherd and named Oedipus (which means 'Swell foot'). Oedipus was taken by the shepherds to the city of Corinth and raised there by the royal family.

Oedipus

Oedipus, now a young man, went to Delphi to learn more about himself and it was here he was told that he was destined to kill his father and marry his mother. Supposing this to mean his Corinthian parents, Oedipus determined not to return to Corinth but to travel. On the road to Thebes, Oedipus encountered a group of Thebans and argued with them. The altercation got out of hand and Oedipus killed the lot of them, the Theban group included their king Laius. Oedipus arrived at Thebes to find the city in turmoil. Not only was the king missing, but the city was being terrorised by a Sphinx, a monster that killed those who failed to answer its' riddles. The first part of Oedipus' fate had been fulfilled.

Oedipus the king

Desperate for assistance Creon, the brother of Queen Jocasta appealed for help. Creon offered the kingship of the city and the hand of Jocasta in marriage to anyone who could rid Thebes of the Sphinx. Oedipus took up the challenge and succeeded in defeating the Sphinx. He answered the riddle and the Sphinx in despair killed itself. Oedipus returned to Thebes in triumph and claimed his prize. Oedipus reigned in peace for many years happily in ignorance that Jocasta was in fact his mother. Oedipus and Jocasta had four children; two sons Eteocles and Polynieces and two daughters Antigone and Ismene. Unwittingly, Oedipus had fulfilled the second part of the curse that was fated him.

Towards the *Antigone*

Years passed and Thebes became subject to a terrible plague. Oedipus enquired as to the origin of the plague and learned that the plague could only be cured by discovering and removing the murderer of former king Laius from Thebes. Oedipus becomes determined to accomplish this act; unaware that the guilty party was himself. Investigating, Oedipus came to gradually realise that it was he himself that had murdered his own father and thus brought the plague down on Thebes through his impious act and also his marriage to Jocasta. Jocasta, horrified at the revelation, committed suicide by hanging herself and Oedipus savagely blinded himself before heading away into exile.

Oedipus and Jocasta's sons Eteocles and Polynieces now assumed power, but it was a troubled time for themselves and the city of Thebes. Since they could not agree when ruling together as joint monarchs, it was decided that each brother should rule alone for a year in turn. Polynieces travelled to Argos and married Argeia, the daughter of King Adrastus of Argos.

Eteocles became king first and Polynieces, realising that his brother would not abide by the agreement and relinquish the kingship at the year's end, decided to seek assistance to take Thebes by force. Raising an army of Argives and Peloponnesians, Polynieces and the other leaders of the army (the Seven Champions) attacked Thebes. The battle was fierce but in the end the Thebans were victorious and the Seven champions were defeated and slain. Casualties at Thebes were also heavy and one of the many killed was Eteocles himself. Polynieces and Eteocles met each other in combat at the Hypsistai Gate and there killed each other.

Creon now became king of Thebes. His first order was to bury Eteocles with full honours, but to also order that the traitor Polynieces' body be left exposed and unburied, Polynieces' rotten corpse was to be eaten as carrion by dogs and vultures. It is at this point that the *Antigone* begins.

The political context of the *Antigone*

Antigone is a play that primarily concerns itself with the *polis*; the city. How should those in power act? Is it right to question their authority? What steps should be taken against those that challenge the established authority of the city?

Sophocles produced the Antigone around the year 443/2BC. The years immediately before and after were a period of tremendous activity and importance for the development of Athens and her empire and also significant for the author of the play himself, as he was closely involved with several of these events.

Athens had recently made peace with Sparta after over a decade of warfare against that city and her allies, notably Corinth and Thebes. In 446BC Athens had narrowly averted an invasion by a large Spartan led army, allegedly bribing the Spartan king to withdraw. This invasion itself had followed upon Athens losing her Greek mainland 'empire', the conquered territories of Boeotia (of which territory Thebes was the principal city state) as well as Megara. Thebes had been defeated in battle in the 450s BC in a series of battles and forced into a form of alliance with Athens.

The loss of both Megara and Boeotia had come about as a result of political exiles conspiring with allies within the cities in order to oust Athenian favoured governments and install a pro-Spartan administration. The problems of the city and how to deal with political exiles was a current problem for Athens, and it is these subjects that Sophocles touches upon in his *Antigone*.

In the year 441BC one of Athens' principal allies, Samos, revolted from the Athenian league. After some provocation by Athens, Samos revolted from Athenian leadership and made her own bid for power. Samos was a strong naval power and it required the vast majority of Athenian naval forces to subdue the island after many months' siege and several battles. One of the generals serving in the campaigns against Samos was Sophocles. Ancient tradition asserts that it was as a result of Sophocles' success with *Antigone* that helped him to be elected general.

The play continued to be performed long after Sophocles' death. The great speech writer and politician Demosthenes used an excerpt from *Antigone* to support an argument on the proper loyalties of citizens.

In modern times the play has been reproduced on several occasions and been adapted to tackle the issues of the day. In the 1940s playwrights Jean Anouilh and Bertolt Brecht both performed the play which portrayed Creon as Hitler and Antigone as either French or German resistance to this leader. History has condemned Hitler because of his actions. Likewise, Creon is condemned by Sophocles' in his play for his actions.

Dramatis Personae in the *Antigone*

Antigone – a daughter of Oedipus

Ismene – a daughter of Oedipus

Creon – Uncle of Ismene and Antigone and king of Thebes

Eurydice – Creon's wife

Haemon – Creon's son and engaged to be married to Antigone

Tiresias – A Blind Seer

Sentry – guarding the battlefield

Guards – for the sisters

Messengers – delivering news

Boy – accompanies Tiresias

The Chorus - Theban Elders

The structure of *Antigone*

The *Antigone* of Sophocles adopts an orthodox structure with no innovative surprises in its' organisation. It begins with a *prologue* (between two characters – which is typical for Sophocles) before the arrival of the Chorus (the *parados*). The play then follows a uniform pattern of alternating episodes and choral odes (*stasimon*), five in number. Finally the play reaches its climax and end in the Exodus.

Robert Fagles' translation of the play, which we shall use as our reference guide, numbers 1470 lines. The breakdown and structure of the play is as follows;

- Prologue (lines 1-116)

- Parados (lines 117-179)

- 1st Episode (lines 180-376)

- 1st Choral Ode (lines 377-424)

- 2nd Episode (lines 425-655)

- 2nd Choral Ode (lines 656-704)

- 3rd Episode (lines 705-878)

- 3rd Choral Ode (lines 879-899)

- 4th Episode (lines 900-1034)

- 4th Choral Ode (lines 1035-1089)

- 5th Episode (lines 1090-1238)

- 5th Choral Ode (lines 1239-1272)

- Exodus (lines 1273-1470)

Synopsis of Sophocles' *Antigone*

What follows next is an overview of Sophocles' *Antigone*.

Prologue (lines 1-116)

Antigone and Ismene sneak out of the palace and here Antigone reveals her plan to bury Polynieces to Ismene. Ismene warns Antigone that Creon will execute anyone who attempts him. Ismene is afraid to help but Antigone is adamant that she will bury their brother.

Parados (lines 117-179)

The Chorus, dressed as Theban elders, enters. They have gathered at dawn to hear Creon's proclamation. They are happy that Thebes has survived the Argive assault but grieve that Eteocles has died.

1st Episode (lines 180-376)

Creon enters and greets the Chorus. He announces what he thinks are good qualities in a king and how he intends to govern. He announces the burial of Eteocles and the exposure of Polynieces and the punishment of any that defy him. A Sentry enters and reveals Polynieces has been lightly covered in dust; an act of symbolic burial. Creon rejects the view of the Chorus that it was the will of the Gods and suspects instead that the guards have been bribed to do it themselves. Creon threatens the Sentry with execution if he doesn't find the culprit.

1st Choral Ode (lines 376-424)

The theme of the first Choral Ode is the resourcefulness of Man and that his skills can be used for either good or evil.

2nd Episode (lines 425-655)

The Sentry has captured Antigone. The guards had caught Antigone attempting to bury Polynieces again after they had exposed his corpse once again. Challenged by Creon, Antigone admits that she has performed this act, and that she was justified in burying Polynieces by obeying the unwritten laws of the Gods. Creon is angered and condemns both Antigone and Ismene to death by stoning. Ismene announces she wants to share her sister's fate, but Antigone refuses her.

2nd Choral Ode (lines 656-704)

The Chorus sing of the cruelty of a curse that can continually destroy a family over several generations. No human crime can escape Zeus' punishment and men can be led to destruction by the Gods controlling man's ambitions and desires.

3rd Episode (lines 705-878)

Haemon enters and submits himself to Creon's will. Creon warns him of evil women and explains why Antigone must die. Obedience is good, whilst disobedience is evil. Haemon informs Creon that Antigone has the sympathy of many citizens in Thebes and that Creon should be lenient. Creon is angered by Haemon and tells him he is acting the part of a woman. Haemon promises that Antigone's death will lead to another death. Creon decides to spare Ismene and entomb Antigone.

3rd Choral Ode (lines 879-899)

The Chorus sings of Eros, the kind of love that is irresistible desire. Desire leads to madness and worse.

4th Episode (lines 900-1034)

Antigone's lament (*kommos*). In this *kommos* Antigone tells the Chorus of her family curse. The Chorus tells her it is her own actions that have led to her fate. Creon orders Antigone to be entombed and declares that he is able to do this without guilt. As she is led away, Antigone imagines she is reunited with her family in death.

4th Choral Ode (lines 1035-1089)

The Chorus compares the fate of Antigone's fate with others; Danae, Lycurgus and Cleopatra.

5th Episode (lines 1090-1238)

Tiresias the Seer enters and tells Creon that he is at fault. Creon is angered by this, but Tiresias persists explaining that Creon is guilty of a double religious crime. Firstly Creon has offended the gods by refusing to bury Polynieces, and secondly he has buried Antigone alive, offending the Gods of the dead. Creon is persuaded and asking the advice of the Chorus, he decides to free Antigone.

5th Choral Ode (lines 1239-1272)

The Chorus pray to Dionysius to cleanse Thebes.

Exodus (lines 1273-1470)

A Messenger arrives to report the suicides of Antigone and Haemon. Eurydice hears the news that her son is dead and departs. Creon enters bearing the body of Haemon and is joined by Messengers reporting the suicide of Eurydice. Her corpse is brought on stage. Creon accepts that his actions have caused all these deaths. The Chorus states that arrogant men who boast are always inflicted with the harshest punishment.

2.2: The Prologue of *Antigone*

Introduction

This topic focuses on the first part of the *Antigone*, the prologue.

In this section we will;

- *Understand the setting and beginning of the play*

- *Analyse the prologue to consider what themes will be raised in the Antigone*

- *Consider some of the dramatic techniques used in this part of the play*

The Prologue

Different Greek tragedians used different techniques to launch their plays. Whilst Euripides often used a single character to begin the play, Sophocles typically used two actors on stage from the very start to begin his plays. This would instantly create dialogue and therefore differences in opinion between the characters.

> **Characters involved in this part of the play;**
>
> - *Antigone*
>
> - *Ismene*

Prologue (lines 1-116)

In this part of the play Antigone and Ismene sneak out of the palace and here Antigone reveals her plan to bury Polynieces to Ismene. Ismene warns Antigone that Creon will execute anyone who attempts him. Ismene is afraid to help but Antigone is adamant that she will bury their brother.

The setting

The setting of the Antigone remains constant throughout. The action is set in one location and does not involve any sophisticated stage machinery. For Sophocles the impact of the play will come from the strength of the characters and the chorus. The scene depicts the grounds just outside the palace doors in the city of Thebes.

The play begins outside the doors of the palace just before dawn shortly after the battle that saw the deaths of both Eteocles and Polynieces. The characters involved in the prologue are Antigone and Ismene. As will soon become clear to the audience, Antigone and Ismene are two very different personalities, with different views on how to deal with Creon's declaration that Polynieces should remain unburied.

Key terms

Rhesis – A set speech by an actor which is characterised by logical argument or ordered reasoning, yet may also include emotional appeal.

Stichomythia – This is a particular kind of argument or dialogue, consisting of a rapid, single-line exchange.

Analysis of the Prologue

In the Prologue the relationship between Antigone and Ismene is outlined and explored by Sophocles. It is also in the prologue that Sophocles lays out some of the key themes of the play, namely should Polynieces be buried and whether the laws of the state of more important than the laws of the gods, and the bonds of blood and family.

In the very first line Antigone stresses her close relationship to her sister Ismene by referring to Ismene as *"My own flesh and blood"* in Fagle's translation, but in the Greek this is literally *"Very sister of common blood"*. The implication here is to state how close the sisters are at this point in the play. The bonds of family remain at the forefront of the dialogue in line four when we read *"For the two of us"*. This line, like the first, stress the closeness of the bond between Antigone and Ismene and by extension their two dead brothers. Yet by the end of the prologue Antigone has abandoned the language of closeness she used with reference to her sister.

By line 9 the dialogue has shifted to Creon and his edict. The first mention of Creon is notable. He is not referred to as Uncle, or even king. He is called Commander (or *strategos* General in the Greek). Creon then is not considered to be family here, although he is. Instead he is called a military leader.

In lines 22-23 we can read that Antigone has drawn Ismene outside. This would have been considered to be unusual to the Greek audience (who would have been almost entirely male). In Athens in the 5th century BC women, especially well born women, would have been chaperoned when in public and to be outside at night would indicate that something suspicious was underway.

Antigone's initial *Rhesis (lines 26-46)*

Antigone begins a *Rhesis* at this point; the focus of this initial argument is Antigone's belief that it is her duty to bury Polynieces' corpse. If one brother, Eteocles is to be buried with honour, then so should Polynieces. A body unburied and un-mourned gives offense to the Gods, Antigone argues and her opinion of Creon is somewhat sarcastic; being referred to as 'good' or 'noble'.

Antigone also produces an interesting statement in lines 44-46;

"There you have it. You'll soon show what you are;

worth your breeding, Ismene, or a coward –

for all your royal blood".

Given our knowledge of Antigone's family and by extension her being the daughter of her own brother (Oedipus) by the same mother (Jocasta), this statement is ironic. Antigone's family is under a curse and although royal, her family is at least unique as for many the offspring of such a relationship would have been viewed as nothing less than monstrous.

The nature of the dialogue now shifts into a brief *Stichomythia* (lines 47-59) Antigone requests Ismene's help in burying her brother. Ismene, however, is reluctant. Antigone stresses it is her duty to bury Polynieces, but Ismene is afraid to go against the will of Creon.

Creon is the *kurios* of Antigone and Ismene. In Ancient Athens a *kurios* was a term that referred to the male authority of a female. The *kurios* could be a woman's father, brother, uncle or husband. It was expected that an Athenian woman would obey her *kurios*. To go against the *kurios* would be seen as extraordinary.

> **Key terms**
>
> *Kurios*
>
> The senior male householder in an ancient Greek society.

Ismene's *Rhesis* (*lines 60-81*)

Ismene's response is to be realistic and to calm her sister. In this she is clearly unsuccessful. Ismene reminds Antigone (and by extension the audience) of the tragic events that had inflicted their family. She also stresses the importance of the city, law, power of the king and the role of citizens and women in maintaining a well ordered city. Ismene accepts that the dead should be buried and not left exposed, but she also adds that she lacks the power to act rightly in this regard.

Antigone replies with contempt to her sister's argument and another brief exchange occurs. Antigone dismisses her sister and her arguments and drops the language of family. Instead Antigone treats Ismene as an enemy now that she knows that she will have to accomplish the burial of Polynieces alone. Twice, in lines 104 and 108 Antigone announces that she will *hate* her sister.

Antigone departs and the last lines are left for Ismene. Ismene announces that despite all their differences, Antigone must not forget that her sister loves her.

Tasks and activities for this section

1) Explore what the Athenian audience would find unusual and interesting in the prologue of Sophocles' Antione?

2) What evidence is there for rationality and irrationality in both the arguments of Antigone and Ismene in the prologue? Present the arguments Antigone and Ismene make as either rational or irrational.

You may want to use a chart such as is presented below;

	RATIONAL ARGUMENT	IRRATIONAL ARGUMENT
ANTIGONE		
ISMENE		

2.3: The First Episode

Introduction

This topic focuses on the first episode of *Antigone*. The first episode (lines 179-376) involves the characters of Creon, the Sentry and interjections by the Chorus and choral leader. The episode ends with a choral ode.

In this section we will;

- *Consider some of the dramatic techniques used in this part of the play*

- *Explore the character of Creon in the first episode*

- *Examine the role of the Sentry in Antigone*

Characters involved in this part of the play;

- *Creon*

- *Sentry*

- *Antigone*

- *Ismene*

Creon: An overview

Creon arrives on stage declaring himself king, not through ability, but because as Uncle to Eteocles and Polynieces, he is the eldest surviving relative. As king, Creon rapidly establishes his intent; to set the ship of state on a steady course. In doing this he will establish the kind of ruler that he is and create he hopes sound policies for the future.

To be fair to Creon, Thebes has had a rather tough time, first with Oedipus and now the strife between his sons that led to an Argive army attacking the city. What Thebes now needs, he argues, is stability balanced with some tough love.

Creon's first act is to declare that Polynieces be denied burial; next he demands loyalty from the Chorus, the Old Men of the city. How Creon is viewed by the people of Thebes is illustrated by the sentry that arrives with the news that Polynieces has indeed been buried; he is scared for his life and it is only with some reluctance and fear of the consequences that he comes to tell Creon of the prohibited burial.

Creon soon demonstrates his arrogance. The gods could never come to bury Polynieces, and Creon cannot believe that this would occur. Instead Creon suspects that there are people within Thebes who could be bribed to commit this act and with no one else to blame at this point, he threatens the sentry to catch whoever was responsible; else *he* would be the main suspect.

When Antigone is captured trying to rebury her brother, Creon heaps scorn upon her. He likens Antigone to a 'rebellious horse' or a 'proud slave'; something that needs its pride humbled. Seeing a conspiracy where there is none, he believes that Ismene is also responsible for this act.

As *Antigone* progresses, Creon becomes increasingly erratic. He even suspects his own son Haemon, believing that, because people are questioning his commands, that they must therefore be traitors. Creon therefore is presented as the worst form of tyrant; harsh, overbearing and, quick to imagine enemies all around him. He is threatening and cruel; he even cuts Antigone off in mid speech despite knowing this is the last time she will be among the living. Rather than be executed, he decrees that she be buried alive.

Likewise when Tiresias arrives onstage Creon first responds to his statements that Tiresias is corrupt and has been bribed. It is only when the blind Seer Tiresias has been insulted and pronounces in turn his dreadful prophecy that Creon's family will suffer, that Creon starts to realise that he may be in the wrong. He attempts to make amends. But by this time it is, of course, too late.

Creon's First *Rhesis* (lines 179-235)

Creon enters the stage with a triumphal, yet aggressive, even arrogant attitude. Creon likens the state to a ship that has weathered a storm. This is a fairly common *simile*.

> **Key term**
>
> *simile – a comparison of one thing to another using 'like'*

Creon has called a council to hear his will. Since Oedipus' sons are dead, Creon is now king. He states that he will put the state first above all other considerations. He decrees that whilst Eteocles has been buried with honour, his traitorous brother Polynieces will be left unburied where he is and be consumed by scavenging dogs and birds as carrion.

Creon and the Chorus Leader (lines 236-248)

The Chorus leader often interjects in Antigone. Here he describes Creon as the possessor of absolute powers. He is a king, an autocrat. An Athenian audience of the 5th century would probably have viewed Creon as someone suspicious. A democracy like the Athenian model had developed from the rejection of tyranny. Creon also introduces his contempt for money and how it leads to corruption – a theme repeated in *Antigone* and an accusation he levels against many of his opponents in the play.

The Sentry

In addition to the Chorus in *Antigone*, Sophocles also utilises not one, but two or more unnamed characters. These additional characters provide the audience with information of events of action off stage and it is their stories that both drive the play forward and also help it to arrive at its tragic conclusion. They also interact with the main characters, no more so than the Sentry does with Creon.

The Sentry enters the stage with some reluctance. He has bad news to deliver and fears the anger that he will provoke when he tells Creon what he has to say. Eventually, the Sentry tells Creon and the audience what has happened out of sight. Despite keeping watch, Polynieces' body has been 'buried', a hasty burial covering the body with dust. The Sentry and other guards at first all accuse each other of performing the burial rites until it is decided to go and tell Creon what has occurred.

As we have seen, Messengers and Sentries are a reporting device of the tragedians, and allowed them to describe the violence vividly, a consequence of their characters' actions, without breaking the taboo of representing violence on-stage. The speeches they deliver take the form of narrative and in *Antigone*, Sophocles uses this device to some success.

The Sentry's tale is interrupted constantly in this episode. As we shall see, interruptions occur frequently in *Antigone*. Here the interruptions are committed by Creon. He is impatient of the rambling story told by Sentry and demonstrates his lack of respect. These interruptions further suggest that Creon is indeed a tyrant.

When the Chorus leader interjects that the mysterious burial of Polynieces was the work of the gods this interjection angers Creon, who embarks on his second *Rhesis*.

Creon's second *Rhesis* (lines 357-376)

Creon roundly attacks the Sentry in this speech. He rejects the idea that the supernatural buried Polynieces. He accuses him of disobeying his commands and threatens him if he does not catch the person responsible. The Sentry must be corrupt or complicit; Creon declares and must have been motivated by greed and money. Money, Creon states, is an evil. This is one of the earliest examples in literature of this common theme.

Tasks and activities for this section

1) *'Creon acts like a tyrant in the first episode'.*
   Write a paragraph length response that supports this statement then another paragraph that challenges this statement.

2) *Consider the character of the Sentry, the message he delivers and the language he uses.*

2.4: The Second Episode

Introduction

This topic focuses on the second episode of *Antigone*. The second episode (lines 425-655) is fairly complex in structure. The episode involves the characters of Creon, the Sentry, Antigone and Ismene and additional interjections by the Chorus and choral leader.

In this section we will;

- *Explore the character and personality of Antigone*

- *Consider some of the dramatic techniques used in this part of the play*

- *Understand and identify the terms Agon and Stichomythia*

- *Explore the characters involved in this episode*

Characters involved in this part of the play;

- *Creon*

- *Sentry*

- *Antigone*

- *Ismene*

We shall consider the narrative of each section below but first we will explore the character of Antigone briefly as she appears in the play.

Antigone - an overview

Whereas Electra is full of self-pity at the start of Euripides play *Electra,* Antigone the daughter of Oedipus, and sister to Ismene as well as the recently deceased Eteocles and Polynieces is defiant and determined. She has a plan; despite the demands of the new king Creon, Antigone will bury her brother Polynieces and ensure that in death he is at least treated with some respect.

Antigone appears onstage on three occasions in the play and on each occasion Antigone has a particular theme which develops the action of the play.

The first occasion (lines 1-116) the Plan *prologos*

It is Antigone who begins the play. Her *prologue* is a determined discussion with her sister Ismene. At first she tries to enlist her sister's support for her plan, but on discovering Ismene's reluctance, Antigone is determined to proceed alone. She determines upon her action in full knowledge of the consequences; consequences that cause Ismene to hesitate. However, Antigone does question whether Creon will actually carry out his threat; after all, *she is* engaged to Creon's son Haemon. By ordering that Polynieces be denied a burial, Creon is dishonouring the laws of the gods.

The second occasion (lines 489-593) Defiance *Agon*

On the second occasion Antigone has been captured by guards posted to keep watch on the body of Polynieces. Consistently Antigone admits her actions, and accuses Creon of challenging the laws of the gods and justice that the dead should be buried and treated with at least that decency. Far from showing fear at this point, Antigone, threatened with death, states that her death will be glorious and calls Creon a tyrant (always a most deadly insult in Ancient Athens). She addresses the Chorus, the Old Men of the city, and declares that they are on her side, but merely afraid to speak out.

The third occasion (lines 895-1035) Antigone's *Kommos*

This is the final appearance of Antigone onstage. Antigone has accepted her fate and now declares that she will be wed to death. Despite being condemned, Antigone does not beg for mercy. She knows that she has done the right thing and would do so again, even if the whole of Thebes would condemn her for her actions.

Structure of the Second Episode

The structure of the second episode is more complex than is typical in a Greek tragedy. It can be divided into four sections;

A) Creon and Sentry (lines 425-488)

B) Creon and Antigone (lines 489-598)

C) Antigone and Ismene (lines 599-631)

D) Ismene and Creon (lines 632-655)

Since Creon and Antigone are onstage throughout a third actor is used to play Sentry and then Ismene.

A) Creon and the Sentry (lines 425-488)

In the first part of the second episode Creon makes few comments. It is Sentry who speaks most. Creon is at first surprised then angered as he listens to Sentry tell how they discovered and captured Antigone trying to rebury Polynieces. Much of the surprise will come from the shock of discovering that it was Antigone; a woman of his own household that dared to disobey him.

The Sentry narrates his tale. He introduces elements of the supernatural – the whirlwind that hides Antigone from view. Sentry also uses several similes in his speech. He refers to Antigone as being like a bird, and the actions of the Sentry and the guards as 'hunters closing in on the kill'. The use of simile was common in epic poetry and a technique used frequently by Homer.

B) Creon and Antigone (lines 489-598)

Creon and Antigone embark on an *Agon* – a set of confrontational speeches.

Antigone's *Rhesis* in the *Agon* (lines 499-524) is focused on establishing the difference between the human laws of mortals and the divine laws of the gods. Creon's laws are outranked by the laws of the gods; even if Antigone is punished for her actions by Creon, she argues that she is still right. Antigone accepts that she must die for her actions but that equally she was obliged to act in order to obey the laws of the gods. Antigone ends with a rather rude remark to Creon that emphasises her lack of respect for him and his laws;

'And if my present actions strike you as foolish,

Let's just say I've been accused of folly by a fool' (lines 523-4)

Creon's response to Antigone (lines 528-554) shows that he has not been persuaded in the least by Antigone. Antigone is stubborn and will submit to Creon's will. Antigone has not only broken the law, but she has laughed about doing so. For Creon, Antigone is acting like a madwoman and is demonstrating her arrogance. Creon also decides to apply more pressure to Antigone. He decides that Ismene should also be punished. That the pair of them must have acted together. This accusation is cue for Ismene to be arrested and brought onto stage.

Key term

Agon *- A set debate, another common feature of Greek tragedy. One character presents his or her case, in a formal manner, and another character refutes the points made. It has the feel of the 'law-court' about them. The aim is to capture the audience through reasoned argument, and since tragedies often represent the clash of two opposing ideologies, there is much food for thought to be found in the agon.*

Stichomythia (lines 555-598)

The pace and tempo of the argument increases after the set *Rhesis* of the *Agon* and is followed by lines of *stichomythia*. Antigone is defiant, she seems to be portraying herself as a hero who like Achilles in the *Iliad*, seeks nothing more than glory and the death that results from this pursuit. She calls Creon a tyrant who does not have the support of the people. Referring to the Chorus, Antigone states that the people obey Creon, not through love and respect, but through fear of him.

Creon in turn accuses Antigone of honouring Polynieces and dishonouring Eteocles. Antigone rejects this charge by stating that Eteocles would understand, but since he is dead, he cannot. Creon distinguishes between patriots and traitors whilst Antigone argues that both brothers deserve a burial. Creon is adamant however and turns his rage on Ismene, who is now brought on stage to take a central role in proceedings.

Key term

Stichomythia – *This is a particular kind of argument or dialogue, consisting of a rapid, single-line exchange. It is not the only kind of dialogue in tragedy, but is of a highly distinctive kind. It serves to concentrate and heighten the emotion or argument, since the exchange frequently takes place between two characters of opposing view-points or of wildly different intentions.*

Antigone and Ismene (lines 599-631)

Ismene tries to share the burden of guilt with Antigone, only to be berated for trying to do so. Antigone refuses to share the punishment she faces with her sister. On the one hand Antigone appears ruthless to Ismene, but it could be argued that Antigone is trying to save her sister's life. Ismene chooses life, Antigone declares, whilst she herself has chosen death.

Ismene appears on stage after Antigone has been condemned by Creon. Creon is seeking to also punish Ismene. The key difference here is that whereas Antigone is guilty of the act of burying her brother, Ismene is innocent of this 'crime'.

Despite this innocence, Ismene tries to share the guilt of her sister. This in turn is rejected by Antigone; she is committed to the act of burying Polynieces and rejects Ismene's attempts to deprive her of some of the 'glory' of this act. However, Antigone does reconcile herself with Ismene to the extent that she desires her sister to live. Ismene is what Antigone would be if she would submit to the will of the city and the laws of men. Antigone however has submitted to the laws of the gods and acts accordingly.

Creon and Ismene (lines 632-655)

The culmination of the second episode is not between Creon and Antigone. Instead it is for Ismene to confront the Theban king. Creon interrupts Antigone and Ismene, declaring that both sisters are mad. Ismene then addresses Creon, whilst Antigone remains silent. At this point, both sisters are still under the sentence of death. Ismene tries to save Antigone (not herself) by taking a new line of attack. If Creon executes Antigone, he will be depriving his son Haemon of his bride to be. This is a twist in the traditional myth of Antigone and a Sophoclean invention. Creon coarsely refers to Antigone as merely a field to be ploughed – a very disrespectful remark to make to your son's fiancée.

Tasks and activities for this section

1) Consider the two characters of Antigone and Creon. What seem to be the driving forces to their behaviour? Consider whether you like or dislike these characters?

2) Sentry spends much of the time in the first episode talking about himself. Why do you think that Sophocles has Sentry act this way?

3) Why do you think Sophocles has Ismene play such a prominent part in this episode

2.5: The Third Episode

Introduction

This topic focuses on the third episode of *Antigone*. This episode (lines 705-878) involves the characters of Creon and Haemon and additional interjections by the Chorus and choral leader.

In this section we will;

- *Explore the character and personality of Haemon*

- *Consider some of the dramatic techniques used in this part of the play*

- *Understand and identify the terms Agon and Stichomythia*

- *Explore the characters involved in this episode*

> **Characters involved in this part of the play;**
>
> - *Creon*
>
> - *Haemon*

Introduction

Although it is not stated in the narrative of the play explicitly, it appears that some time has passed since the Second Episode. This episode focuses on the encounter between Creon and his sole surviving son Haemon. This episode is centred on an *Agon*, as Haemon pleads for leniency whilst Creon is unbending, with the Chorus taking the role of judge. However, the chorus are not impartial, first taking one side and then the other.

As Haemon enters the stage, both Creon and the Chorus expect that Haemon will be emotional and upset that his bride-to-be is to be executed. It is a little surprising then that Haemon's first lines are measured and calm, even warm towards his father. The initial dialogue contrasts well with the remainder of the episode.

> **Key terms**
>
> *Agon* - A set debate, another common feature of Greek tragedy. One character presents his or her case, in a formal manner, and another character refutes the points made. It has the feel of the 'law-court' about them.
>
> *Rhesis* – A set speech by an actor which is characterised by logical argument or ordered reasoning, yet may also include emotional appeal.
>
> *Stichomythia* – This is a particular kind of argument or dialogue, consisting of a rapid, single-line exchange.

This *Agon* is highly structured. Creon and Haemon are each allowed an equal number of lines. Like a law court in Ancient Athens, both prosecution and defendant are permitted an equal amount of time to present their case. The *Agon* of Creon and Haemon then, deliberately mirrors the law court of 5th century Athens.

Both Creon and Haemon begin the *Agon* with a set speech; a *Rhesis*.

Creon's *Rhesis* (lines 713-761)

Creon states that the relationship between father and child is a structured one. The father commands and the child will obey. A good obedient child is a source of pride, whilst a 'useless' child is nothing but trouble for their father. Creon implores Haemon to reject his bride-to-be. He tries to justify his actions; he has to kill Antigone because of her disobedient actions. A man that can control his family is fit to rule a state as well. A man that cannot is not. This is ironic, as subsequent events demonstrate; Creon cannot effectively govern either his family or his state. Creon's speech ends with a warning about Anarchy – a huge danger to both family and city state. The way to avoid Anarchy is to obey the law. The speech ends with an interjection by the Chorus. The king speaks sense. It is now Haemon's turn.

Haemon's *Rhesis* (lines 764-809)

Haemon agrees with the sentiment of Creon's speech at first. But then Haemon relates his observations made as he has wandered about the city (implying that some time has passed). The people of Thebes, Haemon declares, sympathise with Antigone. Haemon states that the people think that instead of death;

'She deserves a glowing crown of gold'.

Sophocles.*Antigone*.782

Haemon urges his father to listen to the advice of others and be more flexible. Haemon uses a metaphor to support his advice to his father. Haemon likens the situation to be like a tree that bends in the winter torrent and again a ship that is caught in a gale. If the ships sails are too taut, they will tear in the gale. Better to slacken them off and to continue sailing, rather than see the sails rip in the strong winds. In his final lines Haemon urges his father to listen to his son and change course. The Chorus then interject. The speech of the son is a wise one and they award equal praise to both parties.

If Creon took Haemon's advice then all will be well. However, this cannot happen in the tragedy. Instead Creon's response to Haemon is anger.

Stichomythia (lines 813-859)

Creon rejects the advice of Haemon. Having already declared Antigone a traitor, he will not listen to the opinions of an infatuated boy. Haemon replies that it is Creon alone who has this viewpoint. The city also desires leniency for Antigone. Creon however is in no mood to listen to the city. Even if the city is correct, Creon is king and it for him alone to decide. Haemon then exacerbates the situation by stating that it is Creon himself that acts like a boy. Haemon continues to press his point. A king must listen to the city. Creon rejects this, insisting that the command if his alone.

Creon turns to the Chorus in disbelief that Haemon is taking Antigone's side and now receives the most direct insult that Haemon can deliver to his father. He likens his father to a woman who should be cared for by his son! Creon is enraged by this. Creon is the king and will not be treated as anything else. Haemon accuses his father of outright tyranny; he offends the gods and justice with his actions and is unfit to be a king. Creon does not seem to be listening. He turns the argument back to the issue of Antigone. Creon decides that Haemon must be her accomplice and does not listen when Haemon states with foreboding that the death of Antigone will lead to another death. For Creon, this is seen as a threat, but actually Haemon is talking about himself.

Haemon has revealed Creon to the audience for what he is. Creon is a tyrant and an arrogant bully who is clearly unfit to rule both his family and his city. Creon has no reply to Haemon's pronouncement except to continue with his bluster and threats; thereby proving his son correct.

The Aftermath (lines 860-869)

Haemon storms out, leaving Creon and the Chorus onstage. They are together in a state of collective shock. Creon declares that he has been at least partly influenced by his confrontation with his son. Ismene will be spared. Antigone however will still die. Instead of being stoned to death by the people of Thebes, Creon instead comes up with a method of execution that is crueller and much more cowardly. Antigone is to be entombed alive with enough food to ensure that her death will come through starvation rather than from any act of Creon's.

This way Creon hopes, naively so, to prevent any pollution affecting himself and the city (line 874) through being associated with Antigone's death. This adjustment in the method of execution acknowledges two things. Creon knows he does not have the support of the people in this act, but also refuses to accept the responsibility for the death of Antigone onto his own shoulders. This decision presents Creon as a tyrant; malicious and at the same time, a coward.

Tasks and activities for this section

1) Having read the above episode, create a table which summarizes the key arguments of the two protagonists; Haemon and Creon with the Chorus interjecting.

2) 'Haemon is the voice of the people in Antigone.' How far do you agree with this statement?

2.6: The Fourth Episode

Introduction

This topic focuses on the *Kommos* of Antigone. She is to be executed and now laments her fate.

In this section we will;

- *Examine the role of the Kommos in Antigone*

- *Consider attitudes towards family and marriage*

- *Explore some of the innovations Sophocles uses to create tension in Antigone*

Characters involved in this part of the play;

- *Antigone*

- *Creon*

- *The Chorus*

Antigone's *kommos*

Antigone's lament or *kommos* is extended and notable not only in that it is interrupted by Creon, but that the choral interjections are spoken rather than sung. She likens her death to a marriage, only instead of marrying Haemon, Antigone will instead wed death.

Key term

Kommos – It is a lament. Often a Kommos is a lyrical, sung, exchange between the Chorus and a character.

Antigone's *Kommos* covers a range of issues and themes, which are pronounced by the Chorus. Antigone announces that she will die unmarried. In Ancient Greece, a woman who died unmarried or without children was considered to have died having never fulfilled her purpose. However, there is an ironic twist here as Antigone declares that she will marry Acheron, the god of one of the rivers of the Underworld.

The Chorus begins by stating that Antigone will go to her tomb while she is still alive. They try to console her by stating that she will die in the way that she willed; a unique way to go with her unique fate.

The Myth of Niobe

Antigone reminds the Chorus of the fate of Niobe, who became a stone through her grief for the murder of her children. Niobe was married to an earlier Theban king – Amphion. Niobe foolishly boasted to the goddess Leto that she had more children than her. Leto's children Artemis and Apollo took offence and slaughtered all of Niobe's children. Niobe, distraught with grief, returned to her native country of Phrygia (in modern Turkey) and was turned to stone on the slopes of Mount Sipylus. The rock face of a waterfall then streamed over this stone. Antigone too sees this fate for herself; to be entombed in stone. The Chorus remind Antigone that since Niobe had immortal blood (as the daughter of Tantalus, a child of Zeus) and that by likening herself to Niobe, the Chorus think Antigone could be bordering on hubris.

Antigone however rejects this in her next lines. She accuses the Chorus of mocking her and rails against the weakness of the people of the city for not standing with her against Creon's harsh law. If they have to mock her, she states, they should at least wait until she is dead. Antigone likens the entire city of Thebes to a *temenos*; a sacred area that surrounds temples. Both the living city and the Underworld will reject her – she has no home on earth or in the Underworld. Antigone also believes that Ismene and Haemon will not mourn her. She is clearly unaware of the confrontation between Creon and Haemon.

> ### Key term
>
> *Temenos - a sacred area that surrounds temples*

Chorus in turn sympathise with Antigone and wonder whether she is cursed, like her father was; at least here they have some common agreement with Antigone. After this choral interjection Antigone again returns to the theme of marriage; this time that of her brother Polynieces to Argeia (which allowed him to lead the Argive army against Thebes) that has resulted in her own fate and the disastrous events of that conflict. Antigone poignantly reflects on how Polynieces' marriage has murdered her own. The irony of these words foreshadows the news of the death of Haemon in the *Exodus*.

Creon has entered the stage again during the *Kommos* and has stood by in silence for a time. Sophocles departs from tradition by having the character of Creon cut Antigone off mid speech. By interrupting her *Kommos*, Creon is denying the condemned even the grace of a final speech with the rough words;

"If a man could wail for his own dirge before he dies,

He'd never finish."

This is a powerful technique and presents Creon not just as a tyrant, but as riding roughshod over all tradition and decency. After Creon's interruption, Antigone's bravery falters. She repeats that she is to go to her death alone, unloved and un-mourned. Creon remains unsympathetic. He repeats that he will be unpolluted by Antigone's' death.

Antigone then recovers some of her former defiance. She is justified in burying Polynieces as much as she was in burying Eteocles. She can now look forward to re-joining her family who await her. She makes clear that she would not have buried her children or husband (had she had them) if it were them in Polynieces' place; for they could be replaced (interestingly Herodotus recounts a similar anecdote). Antigone reiterates that Creon brands her a criminal for fulfilling her obligations to the gods and her family. Creon has also denied her a husband and children, thereby denying her appropriate role and function as an ancient Greek woman.

Antigone declares finally that if her actions were wrong then she hopes the gods punish her appropriately, but if Creon is wrong, she hopes that he suffers no more than her. Antigone departs unrepentant, defiant to the end. Notably she seems to have forgotten or deliberately ignored Ismene. She refers to herself as;

'the last of a great line of kings' (line 1031)

Creon meantime reconfirms his tyranny by threatening the guards escorting her with punishment for allowing Antigone so much time.

> ### Tasks and activities for this section
>
> - *What purpose does the Kommos serve in the Antigone?*
>
> - *How sympathetic do you think the Chorus are to Antigone's plight?*
>
> - *How effective is the use of deliberate interruption in Antigone in this episode and in other parts of the play?*
>
> - *What does Antigone's statement, that she would bury neither child nor husband if they were in Polynieces' place, tell us about Ancient Greek attitudes to family and marriage?*
>
> - *Do you think Antigone is fair to Ismene in this play? Do you think she is justified in treating Ismene as she does?*
>
> - *How consistent has the character of Antigone been throughout the play?*

2.7: The Fifth Episode

Introduction

This topic focuses more closely on the themes of the roles of gods and fate in Antigone. We shall also consider the role of the character of Tiresias.

In this section we will;

- *To examine the theme of gods and fate in Antigone*

- *Consider the key term harmatia and its' relevance to this play*

- *To examine the character of Tiresias in Antigone*

Characters involved in this part of the play;

- *Creon*

- *Tiresias*

Introduction

The prophet Tiresias is a re-occurring character in several Greek Tragedies and *Antigone* is no exception.   He should be considered an 'Archetype' character that, like a god in other Greek tragedies, is brought on stage to bring the play to its climax. Tiresias is the character that directly informs Creon that his actions have fallen short of his intentions and that his actions are to have grave consequences. Tiresias therefore reveals to Creon his *hamartia*.

Key term

Hamartia - derives from a Greek root word meaning 'to miss the mark' or 'to fall short'. In the context of Greek tragedy, hamartia refers to a failing of the central character which brings out the catastrophe. It has sometimes been translated as a 'character' or 'fatal' flaw; but this is to fall short of the true meaning of the word.

In fact, it is not so much an in-grained character fault as more an opportunity missed, or bad decision made which sets up the inescapability and inevitability of the tragic events which follow.

Deux ex machina – literally this means the 'God outside the machine'. This term is used to describe a force offstage that drives the action of the play towards its resolution. This force is something divine and does not necessarily have to be represented by a deity. The deux ex machina can also appear on stage in order to fulfil its role.

Tiresias (lines 1090-1213)

Tiresias the blind seer is brought on stage by a slave boy in order to show Creon the error of his ways. Tiresias addresses Creon straightaway and makes Creon aware that he always gives sound advice. Once Creon confirms that this is the case, Tiresias warns him;

'You are poised, once more, on the razor-edge of fate'

Tiresias' 1st *Rhesis* (lines 1102-1144)

Tiresias recounts events he has participated in recently. An offered sacrifice failed to burn, a sign that the gods are displeased. Further inquiries by the seer revealed that all altars and sacred hearths have been fouled. They have been visited by dogs and birds that have fed on the corpse of Polynieces. This then is the reason for the gods' disapproval and rejection of the sacrifices. Tiresias therefore calls on Creon to make amends, to yield. The use of the word 'yield' is identical to that used by Haemon earlier.

Creon and Tiresias

His first utterances are ignored by Creon, they appeal to his sense of justice and wisdom, but Creon is unsympathetic to this appeal. Creon in his reply (lines 1145-1161) to Tiresias insults him. He calls him a 'fortune-teller' and refuses to bury Polynieces even if it goes against the will of Zeus. In an act of hubris, he says that he will defy the gods and refuses to bury Polynieces even if Zeus' own eagles rip the corpse apart and *'wing their rotten pickings off to the throne of the god'* (lines 1152-1153). This statement is nothing less than blasphemy and graphic. The idea that Zeus' own chosen servants should dispose of the dead body by taking it directly to the very seat of the god is pure disrespect and clearly demonstrates Creon's arrogance.

An argument ensures between Creon and Tiresias (line 1162-1180). Creon insults the seer and accuses him of being motivated by greed and money. Tiresias in turn replies that

Creon is both a sick man, and a tyrant. Tiresias then launches into his second extended speech.

Tiresias' second *Rhesis* (lines 1181-1213)

Tiresias now predicts disaster for the unrepentant Creon. He pronounces that Creon will make amends by the death of his own child. Not only this, but Creon will be pursued by the Furies sent by the gods of the Underworld and these strike Creon down in turn. Tiresias admits he has been angered by Creon and departs the stage leaving Creon and the Chorus to consider the implications of the seer's prediction.

Aftermath

Tiresias' words have the desired response. Creon is brought to his senses by this threat because he knows that the Tiresias always speaks the truth. The Chorus too are terrified by what they have heard. They appeal to Creon, claiming that the seer has never lied to Thebes. Creon admits he too is shaken but is uncertain how to act. In a turn around, Creon asks for advice. The Chorus - through their leader - are quick to give their opinion. They urge Creon to free Antigone and bury Polynieces and to be swift about it. Creon accepts this advice and declares that he will personally free Antigone. Tiresias however never mentions Antigone. His pronouncements clearly make reference only to the treatment of Polynieces' corpse. It is therefore primarily the treatment of Polynieces, not Antigone that has offended the gods.

Gods in Sophoclean Tragedy

Whilst it is typical for the gods to appear on stage at the end of a tragedy, to resolve the action (called 'deus ex machina'), in the plays that survive, it is rare for Sophocles to deploy an Olympian god on stage. In the Philoctetes for example, Heracles is on stage at the end of the play, whilst in Oedipus the King and Antigone the gods are absent from the stage. In another play by Sophocles, Ajax, we have Athena onstage in the prologue.

Common themes for the gods;

- *The will of the gods is prominent in many plays – it is their will that underpins many tragedies.*

- *The gods do not live by the same standards as men. Their deeds and actions often can be seen as unjustified and cruel.*

- *The inability of men to understand the will of the gods is crucial to many tragibe avoided.*

Gods in *Antigone*

Tiresias fulfils the role of a god in warning a central character of impending doom. Sophocles does use gods on stage in other plays, for example in Ajax, but there are no godly characters in Antigone. They are not entirely absent however. They are appealed to throughout by Antigone and the Chorus, and their will is revealed to Creon through Tiresias.

Tasks and activities for this section

1) How effectively is Sophocles presentation of the character of Tiresias in bringing about the resolution of Antigone?

Consider;

- The prophecies of Tiresias

- The response of Creon

Remember to refer both to the language used and the events described.

3) Consider the view that Sophocles takes something away from his play Antigone by the lack of a God onstage. Does the play suffer from the lack of a god?

Consider

- How a God might be used in the play

- Would the play have more impact if Tiresias was replaced by a god towards the end of the play?

- Would the introduction of a god bring about catharsis in the play?

4) Considering your reflections; why do you think that Sophocles rejected using a god onstage in Antigone?

2.8: Exodus

Introduction

This topic focuses on the final part of the *Antigone*; the exodus.

In this section we will;

- *Consider some of the dramatic techniques used in this part of the play*

- *Examine the role of the Messenger in Antigone*

- *Consider the impact of events occurring off stage in Antigone*

- *Investigate the character of Eurydice*

Key terms

katharsis - *gives us the English word 'cathartic', which we use to refer to something with a great cleansing or purging power. The word in the context of Greek tragedy refers to the effect a 'good' tragedy should have on the audience. It should purge the audience of its emotions, by inducing feelings such as pity, anger or fear and allowing the audience a safe place for the expression of them.*

peripeteia - *refers to a (usually sudden) reversal or change of fortune of the central character. Again, like hamartia this is a typical feature of a Greek tragedy. The reversal can be from good to bad or vice versa. Aristotle considered the first, the change from happiness to misery, the more significant for tragedy.*

> *Characters involved in this part of the play;*
>
> - *Creon*
>
> - *Messenger*
>
> - *Eurydice*

The Role of Messengers in *Antigone*

The final part of *Antigone*, the Exodus, begins with a short speech by a Messenger (lines 1272-1291). Sophocles uses the Messenger in a traditional way. He is here to report news of disastrous events that have occurred elsewhere. He reports the news of the disaster that has befallen Creon – but as yet he does not reveal actual details. The audience must wait a little longer to discover exactly what has happened.

A brief dialogue occurs between the Chorus leader and the Messenger (lines 1292-1302) and information is dripped to the audience. It is revealed that Haemon is dead. He has killed himself. The reason for the delay in the details of the death of Haemon and the fate of Antigone is apparent. This news must be delivered first of all to Haemon's mother Eurydice.

This Messenger has an extended stay on stage in *Antigone*. Whilst the Sentry had brought news that Creon was unhappy with, at this point no harm had been done. However the arrival of the Messenger on stage now brings news of disaster.

The Messenger's Speech is typical of those used in other Greek tragedies. The Messenger tells the Chorus an outline of events. It is for Queen Eurydice (who only now appears to us) that the suicides of Antigone and Haemon as well as the attempted murder of Creon are vividly described and graphic. Part of the irony in the events described by the Messenger is that Creon *has* performed the burial rites for Polynieces. This delay allows Antigone the time to commit suicide in her tomb and for Haemon to discover her. Had Antigone not committed suicide, the terrible events of the subsequent deaths would not occur. It is Creon's repentance *and desire to do the decent thing* by the proper burial of Polynieces that causes this fatal delay.

Eurydice

Eurydice has only one speech (lines 1303-1312), and is on stage only briefly. Disturbed from her act of performing rites for the goddess Athena, she hears voices of lamentation which cause her to swoon. Eurydice then emerges from her home to find out what has happened, stating that she *'can bear the worst'*. From what follows, it is clear that she cannot.

Her appearance is something of a surprise, but a necessary one if we pause to consider. As a woman she feels the need to explain why she is outside in the day unattended. She has not been mentioned in *Antigone* previously, but she is required to receive the worst news she can and the revelation of events off stage are now revealed to the audience. We also need to remember, and are reminded now, that Eurydice has already been bereaved; her son Megareus had been killed during the attack of the Seven against Thebes. On receiving the news, Eurydice departs the stage in silence.

The Messenger's main speech (lines 1313-1373)

Now that Eurydice is on stage, the Messenger begins his tale. He reveals that Creon first of all went to bury Polynieces. He is given a proper burial. His remains are cremated and then a mound is raised over the remains. Only after Creon has buried Polynieces does he determine to rescue Antigone. Approaching her place of entombment Creon hears a voice that he takes to be Haemon. The tomb is opened and a horrific vision is revealed to Creon. Antigone is dead, she has hung herself with her own veil. Clutching her corpse is a distraught Haemon. Creon tries to calm Haemon, but the enraged Haemon draws his sword and stabs at Creon; he misses and in anguish of his actions Haemon turns his sword on himself.

The news the Messenger delivers is too much for Eurydice and another death will occur off stage; Eurydice will stab herself at the altar of Athena with a curse for her husband who has brought about the deaths of her children. The Messenger and the chorus leader briefly consider Eurydice after she departs (lines 1370-1387). The Messenger hopes that she'll grieve in private and do nothing rash. The Chorus leader however is not so sure. The Messenger decides to check on Eurydice and as he leaves, Creon arrives on stage

Creon in the Exodus (lines 1388-1470)

Creon arrives onstage either alone, or as is more presumed with attendants, Creon is definitely accompanied however by the corpse of his son Haemon. Creon is now a broken, distraught man and his grief is clear in his lament (*Kommos*).

Creon's *Kommos* departs from traditional tragic laments in that it is interlaced throughout by the speech of other characters. Whilst a *Kommos* was a sung lament, the interruptions are spoken lines. The effect on the *Kommos* is striking. By being interrupted it demonstrates that Creon is truly alone. He has no support from the Chorus; in line 1400 for example; '*Too late, too late, you see what justice means?*' is one of the interruptions.

The Messenger returns during the *Kommos*. Not only is he also unsympathetic, he has more blows to land on Creon. He reports that Eurydice is dead. Eurydice is then brought onstage. She is brought onstage on a *ekkukléma*; a wooden wheeled platform.

Anagnorisis

> **Key Term:**
>
> **Anagnorisis**
>
> Anagnorisis effectively means recognition. It is the point in a tragedy when a character recognises or discovers the true nature of the situation or true identity of another character. According to Aristotle all good tragedies should have a moment of Anagnorisis.

Creon accepts responsibility for the terrible events that have occurred and repents. It is of course too late, the damage has been done. He accepts that he is polluted with the deaths of his own children. In Ancient Greece, to kill a family member was considered to be one of the most unholy crimes that could be committed; due to this pollution, it was of course an appropriate topic for a tragedy and a theme that occurs in other tragic plays; *Electra* and *Medea* to name a few.

Creon repents. He proclaims his guilt and accepts that he acted arrogantly. In the final parts of *Antigone*, Creon prays for his own death and acknowledges that it is his actions that resulted in the death of Haemon as well as Eurydice. Creon however does not get the last word. He departs stage for the final time in the company of the dead and leaves the final lines for the Chorus. The Chorus ends the play with a verdict. They urge the audience to respect the gods and state that happiness comes from wisdom.

There is irony in the end of the play. Creon sought at the beginning of the play to break the stubborn will of Antigone; but breaks himself. He saw Antigone as unworthy competition; but finds himself defeated by her. Creon, who put the state ahead of his family, not only saw his family destroyed, but saw his authority within the state shattered.

> **Tasks and activities for this section**
>
> 1) Consider why Eurydice leaves the stage in silence?
>
> 2) Who is responsible for Creon's downfall? Himself, Antigone or the Gods?
>
> 3) How far do you agree with the view that the play Antigone should in fact be called Creon?
>
> 4) To what extent is there catharsis by the end of Antigone?

Part Three:

Characters and themes in Sophocles' *Antigone*

3.1: The role of the Chorus in *Antigone*

Introduction

This topic focuses more closely on the characters of the Peasant and the role of the Chorus. The Chorus has an extended and important role to play in *Antigone*. They are much more involved in the events of the play than is typical and we also see that the Chorus Leader is almost a character in their own right, interacting with most of the other characters including sentries and messengers. It is also for the Chorus to have the last lines of the play.

In this topic we will;

- *Consider the role of the Chorus in Antigone*

- *Examine and consider the Choral Odes of Antigone*

- *Consider the tale of the Seven Against Thebes*

- *Understand the role of men in the life of the city and the chorus as this role.*

- *Consider the role of the Chorus Leader in Antigone*

The Chorus

In this topic we shall examine the use and language of the Chorus. We will be looking in particular at the entry of the Chorus *(parados)* and the Choral Odes *(stasimon)* of the *Antigone*. The Chorus in *Antigone* are represented as the city elders of Thebes; they are old men from the wealthier section of society. As such it is clear that they are proud of the achievements of their city and initially in a celebratory mood. After all, Thebes has just defeated a strong attack by Argos, led by the 'traitorous' Polynieces.

As is typical in Greek tragedy the Chorus are not present on stage at the commencement of the play. They enter after Antigone and Ismene have introduced themselves and outline the plot in the *prologue*. The Chorus enter the onstage singing a traditional *parados,* the subject matter of which is a Victory Song- given the context of the play this is appropriate- where Argos is likened to an eagle that is driven away by the Theban dragon (an allusion to the mythical foundation of Thebes).

> **Key Terms**
>
> **Parados** – *The entry of the Chorus, the initial entry on stage from the side of the stage. The parados is the first song sung by the Chorus.*
>
> **Stasimon** – *A structured Choral Ode sung with dancing. It bought together themes from the preceding section of the play and explores the moral issues involved.*

Choral songs compared to dialogue between individuals in *Antigone*

Unlike dialogue between characters or the monologues delivered by individual characters, choral songs differ in significant ways. Whilst monologues or dialogue between characters are usually quite clear, choral songs can often be difficult to understand for modern readers. Choral songs in *Antigone* commonly feature mythical allusions which are scattered throughout the play, along with prayers to the gods and references to lands and peoples. In this, the Chorus of *Antigone* is fulfilling its traditional function and role like is seen in other Greek tragedies.

In Euripides' *Electra*, for example, the Chorus is consistently loyal to Electra; however, the Chorus in *Antigone* veer in their loyalties. Indeed they sympathize with Antigone and eventually take an active role in the decision making; instructing Creon to prevent the entombment of Antigone. The Chorus leader in *Antigone* also interacts directly with the main characters quite regularly.

Sophocles keeps his Odes fairly uniform in structure in *Antigone*. Each Ode has four verses, two *strophe* and two *antistrophe,* mostly similar in duration and accompanied by a section that brings the focus of the audience back to the action onstage *(epode)*.

The Chorus is an effective tool used by the tragic playwrights. The Chorus can voice the fears and anxiety of the spectators to an event whose outcome is unknown. They also represent the citizen body in the play, cowed at first by the harsh decrees of

Creon at the beginning, eventually they find their voice and he in turn asks their advice. This is very unusual in Greek tragedy. This then is a depiction of the workings of the polis. Although Creon acts the tyrant, eventually he will obey the instructions of the people as well as the gods.

The *parados (lines 117-178)*

The *parados* in *Antigone* is a victory song providing contextual background to the play and establishing that a victory has been won in battle (something that cannot be directly displayed on stage in this play). The subject matter of the *parados* is the celebration of the defeat of Polynieces and his Argive allies. Polynieces (which incidentally literally means 'Man of many quarrels') was accompanied by an army from Argos led by Seven champions; the so called 'Seven Against Thebes' (see below)

The Argive army is identified by the Chorus by the reference to the 'White shields', it is thought that the men of Argos used shields painted white. Polynieces and his army are collectively likened to an eagle swooping down on the city of Thebes. The eagle is a deadly predator, but is defeated by the Theban dragon; an even more deadly monster.

Several gods are mentioned in the *parados*; Hephaestus the god of fire, Ares, the god of war and Zeus, who represents justice. All three gods are sensible gods to appeal to in battle, especially a battle that occurs at the gates of a city. Zeus supports Thebes in this battle. Polynieces is leading an army that would inflict death and destruction on Thebes.

Zeus hates with a vengeance all bravado,

The mighty boasts of men

Sophocles. *Antigone* 140-141

The reference to Zeus above does not refer to Polynieces, but a different champion in the Argive army. This boastful man was Capaneus who according to the myth boasted that Zeus himself could not keep him outside the walls of Thebes. Zeus proved him wrong by blasting him from the walls of Thebes with a thunderbolt.

The tale of the Seven Against Thebes continues with reference to the *'Seven captains marshalled at seven gates'* (156) and the reference to the *'brazen trophies'* refers to the victories of the Thebans. The brazen trophies were the bronze armour of the fallen enemies that were dedicated to the gods after victory had been achieved. In this case, the trophies are dedicated to Zeus. The brothers Eteocles and Polynieces are the twin spears matched in rage that both win the common prize of death.

The *parados* draws to an end with an appeal to the god Dionysius in the *epode*. This god is doubly relevant. The tragic play was designed for the audience of the Great Dionysia at Athens and was part of the act of worship of this god. Dionysius was also a god that was considered to have been born in Thebes and so was a suitable god for the Theban elders of *Antigone* to appeal to in both these regards.

When Creon enters the stage, his first act is to demand the loyalty of the Old Men of the Chorus. We also see that straight away after the *parados*, the Choral leader is involved in the dialogue and action of the play.

Interlude: The Story of the Seven Against Thebes

After Polynieces had been banished from Thebes, he went to Argos in the hope of finding help in getting restored by the Argive king Adrastus. Whilst at Argos, Polynieces married Adrastus' daughter Aegeia. Adrastus promised to restore his new son in law to Thebes. Another son in law, Tydeus, was also an exile and he likewise was promised by Adrastus that he would be restored to his city. An army marched on Thebes.

The Argive army that accompanied Polynieces was led by seven champions;

- Polynieces

- Adrastus

- Tydeus

- Amphiaraus

- Capaneus

- Hippomedon

- Parthenopeus

Encamped outside Thebes, the champion Tydeus defeated a series of Theban warriors in single combat and the Thebans retreated behind their walls, but not before Creon's son Megareus sacrificed himself to Ares in order to ensure the victory of Thebes. The Argive army then attacked the city, each of the seven champions attacked a different gate. Capaneus who boasted that Zeus himself would not keep him out of Thebes was proved wrong when, scaling the walls, was blasted from them by Zeus with a thunderbolt. Heartened, the Thebans attacked.

Tydeus, Hippomedon and Parthenopeus were slain. Amphiarus fled, but pursued was saved by Zeus who transported him to Hades, to rule as a living king. Polynieces and Eteocles faced each other in battle and both killed each other. The Argive army fled and of the Seven champions, only Adrastus survived.

The sacrifice of Menoeceus is omitted from Sophocles' *Antigone* and is an instance of Greek Tragedians adapting mythical stories to fit the narrative that they desired.

The first *stasimon* (lines 376-424)

There are four verses in this *stasimon* with the *epode* introducing Antigone back on stage after being captured by the Sentry.

The first pair of verses discuss how resourceful Man conquers nature. The earth is presented as an immortal and inexhaustible God, who nonetheless is being worn away by the labours of Man. In the second pair of verses the Chorus sing about how Man developed speech, thought and other skills that result in the creation of a city and civilisation. These skills can be used either for good or evil however, if they are used for evil then the city and civilisation will expel Man. Man's product then; civilisation, is stronger than Man who created him.

There is a warning in this Choral Ode. Balance is precarious. Those who upset the balance through reckless or considered actions can lead to disaster. This warning could at this stage apply to both Creon and Antigone. Since Man's energy can also lead to disaster. This *stasimon* therefore is a foreshadowing of future events in *Antigone*.

The second *stasimon* (lines 656-704)

Like other Choral Odes in Antigone, the second *stasimon* has 4 verses. This Ode's theme relates to how the Gods send ruin to destroy families and cities. This *stasimon* describes the hereditary doom of the family of Oedipus (remember Antigone is the daughter of Oedipus). This tale the Chorus use to remind the audience that Oedipus' bloodline is cursed. Even the young daughters of Oedipus are affected, they are the hope springing up from the late last root.

The Chorus appeals to Zeus in the final two verses. Zeus is all powerful and Man's laws cannot bind this deity. Like in the first Choral Ode, there is a warning in the song of the Chorus;

'Sooner or later foul is fair, fair is foul to the man the gods will ruin.'

Sophocles. *Antigone* lines 696-698

The warning is stark. Actions have consequences which are not anticipated. The Chorus ends this *stasimon* with an *epode* that announces the arrival of Creon's son Haemon.

The third *stasimon* (Lines 879-899)

Again, the Choral Ode comprises of four verses, but the *strophe* and *antistrophe* are shorter, more truncated than the others. Perhaps this indicates that the climax of the play is approaching and is designed to deliver a degree of intensity.

The chorus sing a song about love, not as we as understand the concept of love, but instead likening love as a kind of madness; an irresistible force and another example of the powerlessness of people in the face of greater forces. Not even the gods can resist this kind of love. It causes havoc and madness everywhere it turns. The final pair of verses depict grief and sympathy for Antigone. The Chorus are tempted by love to break Creon's laws and disobey him also. In the *epode* of this *stasimon*, as the Chorus once again draw our attention back to the main plot of the *Antigone*, we see that the Chorus are beginning to falter in their support for Creon. They sympathise with Antigone as she makes her way to her death.

The fourth *stasimon* (lines 1035-1090)

The theme of the fourth Choral Ode requires the most explanation. The Chorus, now thoroughly sympathetic to the fate of Antigone, seek parallels by which they liken her and her fate. They liken Antigone to Danae, Lycurgus and Cleopatra who were all imprisoned in myth. We shall now consider these myths in a little more detail.

The first is the most transparent parallel. Danae was the daughter of Acrisius of Argos. Because of an oracle that foretold that Acrisius would die at the hands of the son of his daughter. Acrisius therefore imprisoned his daughter in a tomb, like Antigone, in order to prevent her from ever meeting a man and having a child. However the barrier of the tomb was insufficient to prevent Danae being visited by Zeus. Zeus visited Danae as *'the cloudburst streaming gold'* and the result was the child Perseus. Perseus and Danae were exiled by Acrisius, but to no avail. He was killed by accident by Perseus years later.

The second parallel is that of Lycurgus. Lycurgus was killed by Dionysius who imprisoned Lycurgus in *'the chainmail of rock'* and subsequently tore him apart with wild horses because he tried to restrict the act of worship of Dionysius in his city.

The final parallel is Cleopatra, daughter of Oreithyia. Oreithyia is an Athenian princess and Boreas a God of Winds. Cleopatra married Phineus, king of the Thracian tribe Salmydessus. When Phineus tired of Cleopatra and married a new wife, he imprisoned Cleopatra and their sons were blinded by the new wife. The final verse is a lament for the fate of the blinded sons which can parallel the pity felt for Oedipus when he learned that he had fulfilled his fate and blinded himself. The theme then is to recount cautionary tales that fate is inescapable. Antigone is doomed. But so is Creon in his way also.

The fifth *stasimon* (lines 1239-1273)

The context of this final Choral Ode is that Creon has finally been persuaded to relent. Surely everything will now be fine? This hymn is dedicated to Dionysius, a god closely entwined in myth with Thebes and also the god in whose honour the tragedies are performed at Athens; the City Dionysia. The first verses of the Ode resemble a classical prayer to Dionysius in order to seek the safety of the city. The god's titles, credentials and most sacred sites are recounted as is Dionysius' relationship with Thebes.

However, the irony here is that all is not well. Dionysius was also the god of madness and irrationality. Creon is about to be struck by the cruel blows of fate himself and his son and wife is to be overcome by grief and madness. The final line is particularly ironic 'giver of good things!' these 'good things' are to be tremendous blows to Creon.

Tasks and activities for this section

1) Consider each Choral song in Antigone (including the parados) explore the subject matter they address and consider the relevance of this material to the play as a whole.

2) Explore what the Athenian audience would find unusual and interesting in the performance of the Chorus in Antigone?

   - You should discuss the participation of the Chorus and the themes they address in the choral odes in Antigone.

3) How important to the plot is the role of the Choral leader in Antigone?

   - You should discuss the participation of and language use of the Chorus leader in his interaction with other characters in Antigone.

3.2: Death and burial in *Antigone*

Introduction

This topic focuses on an important theme in Sophocles' play, the theme of death and burial.

In this topic we will;

- *Explore the importance of death and burial in Ancient Greece*

- *Explore the theme of death and burial as presented in Antigone*

- *Consider the Harmatia of Creon by his action of burying Antigone*

Death and burial in Ancient Greece

The rites associated with burial were an important part of being part of the *polis* or city-state in Ancient Greece. An Athenian of the fifth century had to be able to refer to, and account for, the burial of their ancestors in their *deme* in order to be enrolled as a citizen. Upon reaching adulthood, male citizens were scrutinised by their community in order to assess their eligibility for citizenship. If an applicant could not provide evidence that their parents were Athenian citizens, then they could not become citizens in turn.

Athenian citizens killed in war were often provided with a state burial. Thucydides records a funeral oration allegedly performed by Pericles at the start of the Peloponnesian War. Those bodies that could be recovered were present at the ceremony, whilst those that could not be recovered (perhaps lost on the battlefield) were remembered by an empty coffin.

As we have seen, Athens in the 440s BC (the years preceding the performance of Antigone) saw Athens involved in lots of battles across the Mediterranean, therefore the recovery of, and burial of those killed in battle was of particular relevance to the audience. An inscription of battle fatalities of the Erechtheid tribe (one of ten Athenian tribes) in a single year 460BC names over 150 names. It follows then that approximately 1500 Athenian citizens were killed in battle that year alone. Throughout the 450s-440s Athenian battle casualties each year would have numbered in the high hundreds at least.

The burial rites depicted in the epic *Odyssey*, by Homer, depict how a burial might be undertaken and the importance of correct practice of these rites in Greek thought. For example Odysseus forget to bury Elpenor in Book 10; he was reminded by Elpenor's ghost in Book 11, Odysseus and his men ensure that he receives a decent burial in Book 12.

The situation in epic is not that different to the world of tragedy: the correct rites of burial are especially important in Ancient Greek communities and tragedy after all, were the plays were performed as part of a communal as well as a religious event.

Polynieces

Despite being dead, Polynieces remains a central character. It is the decisions regarding his corpse and whether or not it should be buried that leads to the tragic consequences of the play. Whilst his brother Eteocles is afforded a heroic burial, Polynieces, as a result of being on the losing side is denied even a burial.

In Ancient Greek warfare was customary for the defeated army to request the return of their slain through the use of a herald. It was very rare for this request to be refused and often the defilement or desecration of the dead bodies was regarded as particularly abhorrent. In 480BC, for example the Spartan King Leonidas was killed in battle at Thermopylae by the Persians. According to Herodotus, after the battle the Persian King Xerxes had Leonidas' body beheaded and crucified. This was thereafter held up as a prime example of the savagery of 'barbarians'. For Creon to refuse Polynieces burial therefore he is acting in a barbarous way.

Antigone's burial

Antigone's punishment for performing the burial rites of her brother is at first to be executed by public stoning; this punishment would involve the participation of the citizen body and therefore imply that the citizens would support such a punishment. Once it becomes clear to Creon that the Chorus is wavering in their support for him, he changes the nature of the punishment. Antigone is to be buried alive.

This fate is particularly cruel but Creon has good reason for pronouncing this method of execution. Creon is concerned that he and the city might be polluted by executing Antigone directly. By entombing Antigone and allowing her to starve to death, Creon thinks that he can avoid any pollution of acting improperly in the eyes of the gods. The decision to bury Antigone alive is a classic example of *Harmatia* in *Antigone*.

By acting in this way, the gods of the Underworld are insulted by Creon. By offering a living Antigone to the gods of the Underworld, he incurs their anger and has offended them. The gods of the Underworld did not welcome the living and the act of burial of Antigone meant that Creon was acting improperly towards the gods of the Underworld. This irony is compounded by Antigone's suicide which causes pollution and offense to the gods that was not intended. This brings about the pollution that Creon had hoped to avoid by not executing Antigone in the first place.

Tasks and activities for this section

1) How effectively does Sophocles convey the various feelings towards the dead Polynieces? Consider the opinions of the following characters;

- Antigone

- Ismene

- The Chorus

- Creon

Remember to refer both to the language used and the events described.

2) How effectively does Sophocles convey the various feelings towards the 'burial' of Antigone? Consider the opinions of the following characters;

- Haemon

- The Chorus

- Creon

Remember to refer both to the language used and the events described

Part Four:

Exam Preparation & Further reading

Exam Preparation for A Level

Studying tragic plays – when studying Greek Tragedy at A level the student should consider the following bullet points as you progress through the plays;

- Consider how the narratives and techniques of Euripides differ from those of Sophocles and Aeschylus? For example how do the chorus and actors convey information or display emotion?

- How does the tragedian present themes and issues such as women/society/gods/ justice and revenge/ war and morality?

- Consider the choice of language used in the play – how effectively has the tragedian employed language and dialects used by both the chorus and actors? For example do the characters speak formally or informally? Why do you think that the author elected to use the language they do?

Classical Civilisation - AQA

Candidates taking the AQA A Level in Classical Civilisation;

The AQA unit CIV3C –Greek Tragedy is an A2 level unit and comprises the study of 4 plays as well as the context in which they were produced and performed.

Which plays do I study for AQA?

Any examination candidate wishing to sit the exam in Greek tragedy needs to study the following Greek tragedy plays;

- Sophocles' *Antigone and Oedipus the King*

- Euripides' *Medea* and *Hippolytus*

Understanding the requirements of the exam: AQA CIV3C *Greek Tragedy.*

Candidates will be required to demonstrate knowledge, understanding and the ability to make a reasoned evaluation of the following;

- the structure of the plots
- characterisation
- the conventions and production of tragedies in fifth-century Athens
- the use of the chorus
- dramatic techniques and effects
- the religious, cultural and social context and the place of tragedy in Athenian life, including, beliefs in fate and the gods and the nature of human choice and responsibility, the roles and relationships between, men and women, fathers and sons, mortals and immortals, the concept of honour, attitudes towards the family and city, friends and enemies the nature of political leadership the use of mythology to explore issues of contemporary relevance the values and cultural assumptions implicit in the prescribed tragedies.

The AQA exam unit for this subject with AQA is CIV3C; A study of an aspect of Classical Civilisation 1

The exam comprises 25% of the total A Level and lasts for 1 hour 30 minutes. It is a written examination and is marked out of 75 marks. Exam candidates study one topic from a choice of four. Exam candidates answer one structured, source-based question (from a choice of two) and one extended essay on their chosen topic.

Classical Civilisation – OCR

Candidates taking the OCR A Level in Classical Civilization;

The OCR Unit F384 – Greek Tragedy in its context is an AS level unit and comprises the study of four plays as well as the context in which they were produced and performed.

Which plays do I study for OCR?

OCR periodically make adjustments to which plays are be studied so it is important that you read and study the correct four Greek tragedies for the period under which you intend to sit the exams.

Any examination candidate wishing to sit the exam in Greek tragedy from June 2015 to June 2017 inclusive needs to study the following Greek tragedy plays;

- Aeschylus' *Agamemnon*

- Sophocles' *Antigone*

- Euripides' *Medea and Electra*

Understanding the requirements of the exam: OCR F384 *Greek Tragedy in its Context*.

You are expected to understand the full plot and drama of the four specified Greek tragedies. We shall be making a close, textual study of these tragedies in preparation for the examination.

You will find below further information on each section of the examination for the exam unit F384 *Greek Tragedy in its Context*.

The exam for this unit is comprised of two parts;

Section A

This section is worth 55 marks.

You have 90 minutes available in your examination altogether, so I recommend spending around 50 minutes on this section. In any examination, the number of marks available should dictate the length of time you spend on your answer. The marks breakdown as follows:

- 10 marks are available for factual knowledge of the tragedy (such as knowledge of the events before or after the passage reprinted in the examination)

- 20 marks are available for a commentary on the passage (of around 20 lines) set from one of the four tragedies set. This requires you to examine and analyse the particular linguistic features of the tragedy which you find in front of you, and to understand the effects they are intended to convey.

- 25 marks are available for answering a question on the thematic cross-links that passage has to the rest of the text. You are expected to relate your insight on the passage on the examination paper to your wider knowledge of the tragedy in answer to this question.

Section B

This section is worth 45 marks.

You will have already spent around 50 minutes on section A (including planning time) so you will have 40 minutes to spend on section B. The marks breakdown as follows:

• 45 marks are available for answering an essay question on the tragedies.

Typically, the choice of questions includes some on individual plays (usually not the same as to be found in section A) and the remainder on a study of an important theme going across all of the tragedies studied. You are tested on your ability to relate events, characters and themes across the set tragedies.

The study guide has been constructed with the OCR examination in mind, and you will find particular focus on the varying skills required of the examination as you study.

Drama and Theatre – AQA

In the AQA Drama and Theatre A Level you will be expected to develop your knowledge and understanding of the following criteria for making, performing, interpreting and understanding drama and theatre.

Criteria One

The theatrical processes and practices involved in interpreting and performing theatre. How conventions, forms and techniques are used in drama and live theatre to create meaning. How creative and artistic choices influence how meaning is communicated to an audience. These interpretative processes relating to:

• practical demands of texts
• the choice and use of performance space
• patterns of stage movement
• stage positioning and configuration
• spatial relationships on stage
• performer and audience configuration
• character motivation and interaction
• performers' vocal and physical interpretation of character
• delivery of lines

- listening and response
- playing of sub-text
- development of pace, pitch and dramatic climax
- relationships between performers and audience
- design of sets, costume, makeup, lighting, sound and props
- design fundamentals such as scale, shape, colour, texture.

Criteria Two

How performance texts are constructed to be performed, conveying meaning. The following aspects need to be explored;

- genre and form
- structure
- language
- stage directions
- character construction
- style of play.

Criteria Three

How performance texts are informed by their social, cultural and historical contexts and are interpreted and performed for an audience.

- the social, cultural and historical contexts of plays

- interpretative and performance strategies.

Further Reading

Besides reading this study guide and the tragedies thoroughly, you may wish to read further about Greek tragedy and the tragedians.

Arnott, P. D. *An Introduction to the Greek Theatre* 1965, Macmillan. ISBN 0333079132

Baldock, M. *Greek Tragedy: an Introduction* 1989, Bristol Classical Press. ISBN 1853991198

Cartledge, P. 'The Greek Religious Festivals' in Easterling, P. E. and Muir, J. V. (eds). *Greek Religion and Society* 1985, Cambridge University Press. ISBN 0521287855

Crane, G. *Perseus 2.0* (PIP) 2000, Yale University Press www.yalebooks.co.uk

Cropp, M. J. *Euripides: 'Electra'* 1988, Aris & Phillips. ISBN 085668239X

Easterling, P. E. *The Cambridge Companion to Greek Tragedy* 1997, Cambridge University Press. ISBN 0521412455

Garland, R. *Religion and the Greeks* 1994, Bristol Classical Press. ISBN 185399409X

Goldhill, S. *Reading Greek Tragedy* 1986, Cambridge University Press. ISBN 0521315794

Hogan, J. C. *A Commentary on the Complete Greek Tragedies: Aeschylus* 1985, University of Chicago Press. ISBN 0226348431

JACT, *The World of Athens* 1984, Cambridge University Press. ISBN 0521273897

Morgan, J. *Hellenika Photo CD* 2004, J-PROGS www.j-progs.com

Morgan, J. OCR AS Classical Civilisation OxBox CD-ROM (2008) ISBN: 9780199126606

Morgan, J. OCR A2 Classical Civilisation OxBox CD-ROM (2009) ISBN: 9780199126613

Taplin, O. *Greek Tragedy in Action* 2002, Routledge. ISBN 041530251X

Taylor, D. W. *The Greek and Roman Stage* 1999, Bristol Classical Press. ISBN 1853995916

Online Resources

www.poetryintranslation.com

www.perseus.tufts.net

http://classics.mit.edu/Browse/index.html

www.classics.mit.edu

About Athena Education Online

Athena Education Online is a specialist team of professional course writers based in Lincolnshire, UK. All course writers are specialists in their area and are all are experienced teachers and lecturers as well as experienced examination assessors for the main examination boards, including AQA, OCR, Edexcel and CIE.

About the Author

P Kenney is an experienced, course writer, college lecturer and tutor and examiner for several examination boards. A graduate of the University of Wales and postgraduate of Nottingham University in Classics, History and Archaeology, he has written critical guides for a range of historical and literary texts.

About the Editor

T Kenney is a teacher, examiner and moderator in English Literature and English Language and Literature. She is a postgraduate of Cambridge University and the Open University with a MA in Literature. She has written critical guides for a range of poetry, prose and drama texts.

Terms and Conditions of Use

Thank you for purchasing this product.

By purchasing this product you acknowledge that we the producers of these materials are not affiliated with any educational institution, that this product is authorised by, sponsored by, or affiliated with any educational institution.

Use of this product does not ensure any expected exam grade of anyone owning or using this product. Neither do Athena Online Education guarantee that this product is affiliated with, or suitable for, any particular examination board or examination unit, however Athena Online Education will strive to ensure that all of its products match as closely as possible the qualification for which it is intended to support.

Copyright Information

Disclaimers

Printed in Great Britain
by Amazon